In Season and Out,
Homilies for Year A

T0163939

ISBN
978-1-925371-19-2   paperback
978-1-925371-15-4   hardback
978-1-925371-16-1   ebook
978-1-925371-17-8   kindle
978-1-925371-18-5   pdf

Cover illustration, *The Gift of the Gospel* by Nalini Jayasuriya of Sri Lanka, is owned by the Overseas Mission Studies Center in the United States.

Original lino cut by Yvonne Ashby

Cover design and Layout by Astrid Sengkey

Text Minion Pro Size 10 &11

1. *In Season and Out, Homilies for Year C*, 2015, William J Grimm.
2. *In Season and Out, Special Feasts*, 2016, William J Grimm.

Published by:

An imprint of the ATF Press Publishing
Group owned by ATF (Australia) Ltd.
PO Box 504
Hindmarsh, SA 5007
ABN 90 116 359 963
www.atfpress.com
Making a lasting difference

In Season and Out, Homilies for Year A

William J Grimm

UCAN ·))»

2016

I charge you in the presence of God and of Christ Jesus who is to judge the living and the dead, and by his appearing and his kingdom: preach the word, be urgent in season and out of season, convince, rebuke, and exhort, be unfailing in patience and in teaching.

2 Timothy 4:1-2

Table of Contents

Foreword

The Catholic Church lives on two lungs—Word and Sacrament. They reach their clearest expression and celebration for the Church's life in the Eucharist—the 'source and summit of the Church's life' as Vatican 2 puts it.

Father William J Grimm is a Maryknoll Missioner of 40 years experience in Asia—mostly Japan, but Hong Kong and Cambodia as well. In that time he has come to deepen his understanding of the distinctiveness of the message and person of Jesus Christ even in circumstances and among people that Jesus could never have known or imagined.

Every week for the Church's three year liturgical cycle, Fr Grimm gives visitors to www.ucanews.com—UCAN—the benefit of his learning, prayer, wisdom and experience. Each week, his homilies for Sundays and special feasts are seen by some 3,000 visitors to the main UCAN site and with subtitles on UCAN's Vietnamese and Chinese sites.

We are delighted to offer the texts of these pastoral homilies.

Michael Kelly SJ
Publisher

www.ucanews.com

First Sunday of Advent (A)

When a race starts, is the waiting over, or has it just begun? How about a theater performance? A concert? A football game?

In one sense, the wait is over. When the starting gun fires, the curtain goes up, the baton comes down or the ball is kicked, the participants can at last do what they have come to do. The tense build-up is ended, the action has begun.

In another sense, though, a new wait has begun. Now, there is an action wait, a doing wait. Who will cross the finish line first? How will the play work out? Will the concert be a success? Which side will win the match?

Waiting for the result is common to the participants as well as to the spectators or audience. When it comes to waiting, all are engaged in the same activity. Beginnings mark a new wait.

With the first Sunday of Advent, we begin the Church's season of waiting.

What kind of wait is Advent? For those to whom it is the Christmas shopping season, this is a build-up season. Excitement builds as we wait for the feast. Once it comes, the waiting is over. We put away the Advent wreathes and calendars. The celebration begins.

But, perhaps Advent is about the other kind of wait, the doing wait, the moving wait, the heading toward a goal wait. Perhaps it is more like riding on a train than like sitting in a theater before the show starts.

Actually, it is both kinds of waiting, but backwards. We are not waiting for something to happen and ready then to wait and see it through to completion. We are waiting to see how things already begun will turn out, but we are also waiting for something to begin. The activity is in progress. The onset is yet to come.

What is it that we await? I am living my life day to day, making a story the end of which is still unknown. I am the lead character of my life and I am waiting to see how the story of my life forms a plot.

Of course, since I am the chief actor of the story, my waiting is not a mere 'waiting around.' I am like the actor, the musician or the athlete who is fully involved in the process.

Like theirs, mine is not a solo performance. Others are involved, most of them people I do not even know. There are my family and friends. There are the people whose work makes my life what it is: farmers, engineers, miners, journalists, transport workers, civil servants, etc. There are even the dead, men and women of the past who made the world in which I live, the world that has shaped me, challenges me and supports me.

They are part of my waiting to see what my life means. They wait with me because part of the meaning of their lives is linked to mine, as the role of each character in a play is defined by the other characters.

How our lives intersect is a mystery to us all, a mystery that will be answered by the other wait, the onset wait.

The onset for which we wait is the one we pray for in the Lord's Prayer: 'Thy Kingdom come.'

The coming of the Lord to bring the completion of the Reign of God will give the meaning to the waiting I live today. Just as a race is defined by the finish line (100-meter dash, marathon), so, too, is my life. The run is good in itself, but is fulfilled in the finish.

That finish takes two forms. The most obvious is the end of my life, when my run ends. The other is one that gives the ultimate meaning to my life, the coming, the advent, of the Lord as judge and ruler of the universe at the end of time.

In that, the mystery of all the people and events of all our lives will become clear. So, we 'wait in joyful hope' for the ongoing completion of our own story and 'for the coming of our Savior, Jesus Christ.' Advent is a time to remember that we are waiting and to examine the way we wait, both in loving activity today, and in hope for the future.

Second Sunday of Advent (A)

The first people who took the trouble to go into the desert and look for John returned home and told others about the man in the wilderness who lived on bugs and honey and dressed in camel hair. They also told how abusive he was, attacking some of them for coming in the first place: 'You brood of vipers! Who warned you to flee from the wrath to come?'

And what happened? Did folks say, 'That guy has been out in the sun too long—he's crazy, and maybe even dangerous?'

No. John became a celebrity! 'At that time Jerusalem, all Judea, and the whole region around the Jordan were going out to him.'

Did folks like to be abused? Is that why they made the dangerous trek into the desert? Did they go out of curiosity, to see the wild man in the wilderness? There may have been another reason for their going: they knew John was right.

The psychiatrist Karl Menninger wrote a book titled, *Whatever Became of Sin?* It was a good question. A growing understanding of the psychological causes that lie behind many of our actions, combined with a reaction against a spirituality that seemed to make an awareness of sin rather than of God's sin-forgiving love the center of the Christian life seem to have decreased some of our consciousness of sin.

There is much good in this tendency. Sometimes we are not fully responsible for our actions because of psychological or social factors that influence and even control us. In addition, instead of weighing our consciences and trying to keep mental or even written lists of sins to take to the confessional, we have come to a deeper appreciation of God's forgiving love embracing us at all times.

However, I sometimes move from there to a sort of self-forgiveness. I decide that sin is not a reality in my life, that none of my problems are due to sin—mine and the world's. I sometimes forget that God's forgiving love is precisely that—*forgiving* love. In 'what I have done and in what I have failed to do,' there is something that requires forgiveness.

John's problem with people who went to the desert was not that they were sinners. His problem was that some of them seemed to think that all they had to do was go through the motions. They would admit to being sinners (the more vaguely, the better), go out to the desert for John's baptismal ritual, and then get back to living as they always had.

John warns such folks, 'Bear fruit worthy of repentance. Do not presume to say to yourselves, "We have Abraham as our ancestor."' He then speaks about 'the one who will follow me.'

John moves his listeners from focusing on past sins or present hypocrisy to the future, the time of hope.

'Advent' means 'coming' and coming is something that happens from the future. At this time of year I remind myself that my whole life is lived in expectation of something that is coming, and that does not merely mean December 25.

I have a past and a present. They have made me the person I am. However, the story of my past and present is not the real story of me. My real story is in the future, in God's call to draw closer and in the opportunities (including death) that will bring me closer and closer to God. God calls to me out of the future rather than pushing me from the past.

Every moment is an advent. In every moment God invites me to move away from the past and the present into a new future.

But, there are obstacles. My obstacles are those that brought people to John in the desert, the sins of my past and my tendency to not let go of them in the present.

They prevent my meeting the advent of the future because one of the characteristics of sin is that it is directed to the present. I sin because of what I want to have or want to avoid in the present.

The people who went to the Jordan River had to repent and abandon their sins if they were to meet the one who would come, Christ. The same is true of me. That does not mean abandoning the present. It means living a present that can worthily come with me into the advent of the future. The eternal future to which God calls me must shape my present.

Third Sunday of Advent (A)

Some people want God to be vengeful. Some even appoint themselves the instruments of that vengeance. Of course, such self-appointed condemners and avengers for God seem insensitive to their own sins and their own need to repent.

They forget or ignore what St Paul said about vengeance: 'Beloved, never avenge yourselves, but leave room for the wrath of God; for it is written, "Vengeance is *mine*, *I* will repay, says the Lord."' In other words, 'mind your own business.'

People who think God is about vengeance do, however, have a precedent in John the Baptizer. In last week's reading from Matthew, John launched into a tirade against the Pharisees and Sadducees for trying to 'flee from the wrath to come' and said that 'every tree that does not bear good fruit is cut down and thrown into the fire.'

When Jesus came speaking about beatitudes and hope, John naturally had doubts about him. Shouldn't the message of 'the one to come' be an intensified word about God's wrath that is drawing near? So, John sent some of his disciples to question Jesus. 'Are you the one who is to come, or are we to wait for another?' The answer they brought back may have only increased John's doubts.

'Well, John, we asked him what you told us to ask, and all he said is that good things are happening. The blind receive their sight, the lame walk, the lepers are cleansed, the deaf hear, the dead are raised, and the poor have the good news brought to them.'

And John said, 'You're sure he said nothing at all about the wrath of God? Nothing about punishment for sin and evil? How can he be the One? Didn't I say the one to come will burn the chaff with unquenchable fire? Well, then, he must not be the One.'

'By the way, John, he did say one more thing: "Blessed is anyone who takes no offense at me."'

The kingdom of God is 'righteousness and peace and joy in the Holy Spirit,' says St. Paul. Like it or not, we are called to joy. The Gospel really is good news; the coming of the Lord is healing, peace and reconciliation.

What, then, is the task of the followers of the Lord? Are we to keep quiet in the face of sin and evil? No. I should combat sin, beginning with the sin in my own heart. In addition, I must shine the light of God's will on the sin of the world, that of individuals, of groups or of the entire world—especially, perhaps, those groups and those parts of the world that support my livelihood or comfort. But, I must do all that out of love for the sinner—whether myself or others.

Christians are supposed to be signs of the Kingdom, of the coming of the Lord. That means more than putting up a Christmas creche or even a cathedral. It means more than spending an hour each week in a building with a cross on the roof.

Being signs of the Kingdom means that we imitate Christ. Someone who looks to us to find out if God's Kingdom has come in Christ should be able to see that the sufferings of the world are relieved, that the causes of suffering are banished, that new life is given to all, that the good news is proclaimed to the poor. We should be able to reply as Jesus did.

John tried to live as a prophet of God as he understood God. A wrathful God should have wrathful prophets. So, John was 'hellfire and brimstone.' We try to live as signs of God who is present to us in Jesus Christ. So, we show the forgiving love of God to the world. That is where we are greater than John. We are not better than he; we merely know something about God that John did not know, that God would rather go to the Cross than inflict wrath on the world.

Now as we practice the carols of 'peace on earth, good will to all' it is time to renew our commitment to live as Christ who came not to condemn sinners, but to embrace and save them. That's good news for the whole sinning world, including me.

Fourth Sunday of Advent (A)

There was nothing extraordinary about the name Yeshua that Joseph was ordered to give the child. There were probably other kids in town with the same name. As the Aramaic version of Joshua, it was a popular name.

(This might be a good point to make a little digression into the question of how 'Yeshua' came to be called 'Jesus.' The language of the early Christians outside of Israel was Greek. That is the reason the New Testament was written in Greek. Now, when Greek speakers wanted to speak of Yeshua, they had two problems. For one thing, they had no sound in their language that corresponds to the one we write 'sh' in English. The closest they could manage was an 's' sound. Another problem was that to Greek ears, 'Yesua' would sound like a woman's name, since names ending in 'a' were feminine. Since Yeshua was a man, they changed the last sound to a masculine ending, another 's.' So, in Greek, Yeshua is called Iesus. When Christians moved into the Latin-speaking world where a different alphabet from the Greek was used and where 'I' and 'J' were interchangeable, we got Jesus. The hard 'J' pronunciation in English comes from the fact that in English, we pronounce 'J' and 'I' differently.)

So, Joseph was told to name the child Yeshua, and we name him Jesus. But, that is only one of the names by which we call him. The name Yeshua sounds similar to the Hebrew and Aramaic phrase, 'he will save,' and so the angel said, 'you are to name him Jesus, for he will save his people from their sins.' That is something else we call him. Jesus was one man who was really true to his name, a savior.

His disciples called him 'Rabbi' or 'teacher.' The Church has called him 'Christ' and 'Lord' and 'God-Man' among other titles.

Today's Gospel passage, applying to him a verse from Isaiah (another variation on the same name as Jesus) calls him 'Emmanuel, which means "God with us."'

But, when all is said and done, perhaps the best title he has for us is the simplest, the one his parents and playmates used in Nazareth, the one his disciples used on the road, the one the Romans put on his cross: Jesus.

Think about your own name or the name of someone you love. Is it a mere word, a few syllables that provoke no more response from you than any other sound? No, a name is special. When I say that I am So-and-so, I mean more than when I say I am a jogger or a stamp collector or a bank robber. My name *is* me.

If I say your name, I say a word that carries with it all I know about you and all my feelings about you. I mean not merely one of many human beings, but one who looks and sounds a certain way, has certain interests, does certain things. Your individuality is captured in your name.

And that brings us back to Jesus and his name. In one sense, it is not a special name. It is not unique. Many people had the same name. In Spanish-speaking societies, many people still have it.

That is part of the wonder we are preparing to celebrate at Christmas, that God has become present among us not in some unapproachable, exalted way, but as someone with a name, an ordinary name because that extraordinary man is in a real way as ordinary as you and I. Jesus really is a normal human being with a normal name.

And when I say that name I declare my relationship with him, my beliefs about him, my hopes in him. By saying his name, I say that it is possible for me and other normal human beings to know him and to call upon him with the same familiarity as his playmates in Nazareth two thousand years ago. He is God, but he is also my friend.

The one whose birth we are about to celebrate has many titles, but one name, the name he shared with so many other people in his land. It is wondrous because it is so common. The mystery that we celebrate in his birth is that the God of the universe is met in someone like us, someone with a simple name, an ordinary Tom, Dick or Yeshua.

Holy Family (A)

I saw a picture of the Holy Family that showed Joseph doing carpentry while Jesus held a tool and Mary watched at the door, doing nothing. Not like any family I know.

We know what real families are like. In a real family, Jesus would have been getting in his father's way or been off somewhere else when Joseph wanted help. Mary would have been working at keeping the house livable and the family fed.

If that picture of Joseph's workshop is of a holy family, we're all out of luck. All we can do is look on wistfully, and think how nice it would be if our families were perfect. If family holiness is some impossible situation of goodness, harmony, cleanliness, comeliness and industry, there is no reason for us to celebrate this day.

Perhaps the picture was wrong. Maybe Jesus was a pest around the house. Maybe Mary shouted herself hoarse calling him to meals. Maybe Joseph got so caught up in his work that Mary and Jesus stood at the workshop door, ignored. Maybe Mary sometimes burned the bread.

We have just celebrated the birth of Jesus. The mystery of the Incarnation is that Jesus was not God's play-acting at being human (that's a heresy called 'docetism'). Jesus really was human. He really needed to be toilet trained, he really got bumps and bruises roughhousing with friends. He really could be a pest. He really could be a precious son. The family we call the Holy Family was not all that much different from other families.

Are we wrong, then, to call it a *holy* family if it was no more 'holy' than our own?

Because of the Incarnation, holiness cannot be other-worldliness. The place where God is met, the place where God loves us, is here, now. A truly holy man or woman lives in the here-and-now, is a sign here and now that God's love is real and at work.

The word 'holy' comes from the word 'healthy.' Holiness is a kind of health, and health may be the means for us to understand holiness and, therefore, what we celebrate on this feast of the Holy Family.

When I am healthy, I am able to move through life with a certain confidence. I feel that nothing the world brings me by way of challenge can overwhelm me.

Holiness, too, is a kind of confidence, a conviction that God's love embraces me. God's love is stronger than sin, stronger than death, and so I can live with confidence. I need not fear to love others or be loved by them. I need not fear the world and what it may do to those who serve. I need not fear the power of sin or death.

Think of people who make health an object of life. Besides being burdensome to the rest of us, they are neither happy nor truly healthy. That is because health is a by-product of a certain kind of life. One who walks, runs, dances, or climbs for the joy of it is healthy. One who walks, runs, dances, or climbs for the sake of health is unhealthy.

Holiness, too, is a result, not an objective. When I am filled with amazement at God's great love, when I share that love with all I meet, I become holy. I pray with joy, with gusto. If I turn prayer into some sort of spiritual calisthenics, I will be neither happy nor holy. I will not be a sign of heaven to the world.

That brings us back to the Holy Family. It was holy not because it lived an exalted life unavailable to the rest of us. It was holy because it was a group of people not unlike ourselves who loved, who lived, who wept, who laughed. Theirs was a home in which a boy could 'grow in size and strength, filled with wisdom, (with) the grace of God on him.'

Our homes can be the same. Perhaps more than we realize, they are. They have their problems. No family is without them. Every mother feels swords pierce her heart at some time or other. Yet, our homes are where we learn to love, where we learn of God's love. It is in our families that we practice the sharing, openness and patience that enable us to show the glorious love of God to the world.

Epiphany (A)

Those astrologers or wise men from the East have picked up a lot of baggage on their journey through the centuries. First, they got a number—three—though Matthew says nothing about how many there were. As time went on, they got kingships because the psalm we pray today as a responsorial speaks of kings bearing gifts. They got races and even, eventually, names: Melchior, Balthasar and Gaspar. In 1248, construction began on one of the world's most beautiful buildings, Germany's Cologne cathedral, to house a gold casket that supposedly contains their relics. Sometimes, it seems they have so much baggage that we can no longer see who they are.

So, who are they? What is this special celebration today all about?

Literally, an epiphany is a showing. That's a hint of what this day is. Epiphany is a celebration of the showing of Christ to some very fortunate people: us.

Jesus was born of Jewish parents in a Jewish town, a Jewish boy who grew to be a Jewish man. Why would the birth of Jesus mean anything more to the greater world than the birth of any other Jew? Even granting him to be the incarnate presence of God on earth, of what significance would that be to those who are not themselves members of the chosen people, the Jews? Other great acts of God for that people did not particularly help others. Moses lead the Hebrews through the sea, but it was not the best thing that ever happened to the Egyptian chariot corps. The good news promised to the Jewish people and fulfilled in the coming of Jesus could have been exclusively theirs.

What we celebrate today is the wonderful love of God that did not limit itself to a single people. Jesus came to and for the Jewish people. But he also came for all of us who have no natural ties to that people.

Were that not the case, most of us would not be followers of Christ. Most Catholics, most Christians, are not Jews by descent. We are Chinese and Cheyenne, Maoris and Magyars, Americans and Armenians, Thais and Tlingits, Indonesians and Ibos. We are everybody, and we all bring to the Church our own ways of being Christian, our own colors, to add to the caravan.

That is what we celebrate today, what we give thanks for today. God has chosen to love us, the unchosen people.

The centuries God spent, the prophets God sent, were all meant to build a people within whom a savior could be born for all of us. On Epiphany we celebrate the fact that Christmas was not just for one people, Christmas is for all.

So, who are the wise astrologers? They are all of us. We are the strangers who come from afar, from outside the chosen people, to worship the king of the Jews. We come to Christ, conscious that we have no right to him, and grateful that God's love is not hemmed in.

We, like the astrologers, come to worship. We have seen the signs and wonders of Christ, and recognize and worship him as God among us. We don't bring the gold of a king, the frankincense of a god or the myrrh of the dead, but we worship him nonetheless as our ruler, our God, the One who died and rose. We bring the gifts of our personalities, our cultures, our histories, our traditions and even our sins. We also show the way and invite others to join us as we go to worship the Lord.

On Epiphany, we thank God for the gift of Jesus Christ, a gift given to all of us throughout the world, throughout time. Like the wise astrologers, we respond by bringing our gifts to the Lord: our ways of praying, our ways of singing, our ways of thinking, our ways of acting. Let us give thanks today, too, for each other, for the variety of gifts our fellow travelers bring as 'bearing gifts we travel afar.'

Baptism of the Lord (A)

Once the Church moved beyond Aramaic-speaking Palestine, the language of Christians was Greek. So, Christians used Greek words to describe themselves and what they believed.

Some of the earliest surviving Christian writings are graffiti, pictures and sayings scratched on ancient walls. Among them are pictures of fish because the Greek letters of *ichthus*, 'fish' begin the five words that make up the Greek statement, 'Jesus Christ, Son of God, Savior.'

But the popularity of this image was not merely due to a word game. There was a message in it as well. Fish are born and live in water. Christians, too, come to new life in the water of Baptism. So, the fish symbolizes those who say 'Jesus Christ, Son of God, Savior' and who live because of the sacrament of Baptism.

Some fish are beautiful. Some are grotesque. When they are in water, they generally move gracefully and even the most grotesque have a certain beauty. Out of water, they flop around, their colors fade, they die. If I separate myself from Jesus Christ, Son of God, Savior, I become a fish out of water. I will lose my true beauty and gracefulness. A Christian's true self is a fish self.

What kind of fish? Perhaps the finny fish that best symbolizes Christian fish is the salmon. A salmon is born in water and then the water carries it out into the vast sea. There, the salmon wanders and grows until the time comes for the big event of its life, the return to the place where its journey began.

When I was baptized, I was born as a new creature. God looked upon me, as upon Jesus, and said, 'This is my beloved child with whom I am well pleased.' That was the beginning of my journey of faith. My baptized life has carried me into the great sea of the world, and I have grown as a member of my species, the Christian fish.

Some day, I will return to the point at which I started, and I hope that God will say, 'Here, once again, is my beloved child, worn with the journey of life, coming now to the fulfilment of the union with me that started in Baptism. I am well pleased.'

I am a fish; I am something else as well. The baptism of Jesus was a declaration of his sonship. In that baptism, God declared who Jesus was. The same happened less dramatically, but no less really, in my own Baptism. When the water shows us to be fish, the sacrament declares us to be beloved sons and daughters of God.

That has implications for our lives. When God declared Jesus to be 'my beloved son,' his ministry and his journey to the Cross began. Baptism is not merely a ritual that happens once for all. It is a beginning and a responsibility.

It is a responsibility because we have it in our power to make God look like a fool. God has declared us to be sons and daughters. The world, then, is right to look for some family resemblance between us and God. We should be loving, serving and forgiving, not because that is the way to earn God's favor, but because that is how we are true to the favor we have already been granted.

If we fail to resemble our Father, then God's hopes are thwarted. The life of Jesus declared at every point that he was the true *ichthus*, Jesus Christ, Son of God, Savior. God says that we can be fishlike, that we can imitate Christ. How like him am I?

In today's reading from the Acts of the Apostles, Peter tells the crowd what they can expect of fish people, followers of Christ who 'went about doing good and healing all who were oppressed by the devil.' We should do likewise.

It isn't hard to find good that needs to be done. It isn't hard to find the oppression of evil. We must be willing to swim into the mess of the world and show that God's life can be lived there.

The sea looks like a forbidding place, yet that is where fish live. The world can look like a forbidding place, yet it is a natural habitat for those who have been made fish in the water of Baptism.

Second Sunday of the Year (A)

Ordinary Time in the Church calendar has nothing to do with the humdrum, the everyday. It refers to the fact that we use ordinal numbers (first, second, third . . .) to count the weeks.

Though this is right from a historical and linguistic point of view, the fact of the matter is that we really are in a humdrum, everyday period of the year. Christmas is past, Lent and Easter are weeks away. We are in a 'same-old, same-old' time when nothing dramatically different goes on in the worship of the Church.

It is the most important time of the year.

John the Baptizer said, 'I myself did not know him, but I came baptizing with water for this reason, that he might be revealed to Israel.' In other words, John's whole vocation was meant to point to Jesus, but when Jesus was actually standing right in front of him, John did not recognize him. It took a vision of the Spirit descending from heaven like a dove to make John see what was before his eyes. How can he have missed what was most important to him?

The answer might be 'ordinary time.' John was going about his business, doing what he always did. Granted, standing at the Jordan River wearing camel skins, eating locusts, preaching and baptizing might not be our idea of ordinary, but they were the ordinary things of John's life. The day Jesus came to him to be baptized was a day like any other day.

When Jesus showed up, he was just one more of the people who came to John. John might have been tired, distracted or bored. He was not alert. So, John baptized Jesus as he had baptized many others. Nothing special, just the ordinary. Why should it have been otherwise?

We fall into a routine, and even resent anything that might upset the patterns of our lives. We like each day to be pretty much as the day before. We neither want nor need surprises. We like to live in ordinary time. We like it so much that even if something out of the ordinary were to occur, we might not notice it. Jesus came to John to be baptized, and John did not notice.

But, the ordinary times of my life, are not necessarily enemies. It was in his ordinary time, after all, that John met Jesus. It is in ordinary time, in the day-to-day of my life, that I, too, encounter Jesus. That is the reason ordinary time is the most important time of the year.

The Christian life is not about doing good deeds or conducting beautiful ceremonies or saying fervid prayers or preaching the Gospel or thinking profound thoughts. It is about growing in love of God through Jesus Christ. All the rest comes along with that as aids to that end and results of it.

In the Incarnation, God has come among us in order that we might have that relationship. That coming was not in drama or in power. It was in the life of a carpenter who walked the roads with fishermen—an ordinary man with ordinary people in an ordinary time.

That is when and where we, too, can meet him. My day-to-day life is the place where Jesus is.

Spirituality is not so much a matter of prayer as of awareness, about sensitivity in ordinary time to the ordinary events and people around me. Christ is there among them as he was among the events and people of Israel two thousand years ago. Prayer can and should help me become more able to see God at work in my ordinary time, lest like John I miss seeing Christ as he stands in front of me in the people and events of my life.

And so, the ordinary is, in reality, the extraordinary. There are no ordinary times. There are no ordinary places. There are no ordinary events. There are no ordinary people. There are no ordinary lives—not even my own. Christ the Lord is in them all, calling us, encouraging us and enabling us to know, love and serve God.

There is, then, no need to search for God. Rather, as the Jewish theologian Abraham Heschel said, God is in search of us. God saves me the trouble of the search by coming into my life, into my world. Meeting Christ is the most ordinary thing there is. I can't avoid it, only ignore it.

Third Sunday of the Year (A)

If we look at what Matthew says about the ministry of Jesus, we can see many things that would have caused him problems had he tried doing them as a Christian.

First, he does not stay put. Standard wisdom tells us that anyone trying to build a Christian community should stay in one place, working with people, working on people, working through people to build up an effective public presence. Buildings must be erected, programs must be initiated, committees must be appointed, leaders must be chosen and trained. Jesus failed to do any of this.

Then, there is the way in which Jesus invited people to discipleship. He apparently just picked people at random 'as he was walking along the Sea of Galilee.' No catechumenate or RCIA, no novitiate, no testing, no training, no retreats or seminars. Just, 'Come after me.'

The biggest problem, however, would be what he failed to do. Though he did tell some people to follow him, he did not tell most of those he met to follow him or join a new community of faith.

He did not tell them to abandon the religion of their ancestors. He did not tell them to go and do anything. In most cases, he merely told men and women that the kingdom of God, the fulfilment of God's will for creation, was at hand, and then he went on his way with the small group he had invited to come along. Even after performing miracles for people, he simply sent them home.

Matthew's Gospel is, more than the others, concerned with what the Church should look like, what sort of community of faith it should be. Right at the beginning, it challenges what most of our communities of faith are and what we expect them to be.

Looking at our structures, our hierarchies, our parishes, our congregations, our orders and our organizations, and then looking at the billions of people whom we are not reaching with the Good News of God's Reign, we can only feel uncomfortable. Can it be that we are going about it all wrong?

In one sense, Jesus had an easy time of it. He had no Church that needed all these things in order to carry out its activities and vocation. We do not have that luxury he had. There is a Church; we are that Church. We have to learn to live with it and in it and proclaim the Kingdom through it. Without it, neither we nor the rest of the world could know the Good News. And yet . . .

We will never find an ideal form for our life as Church. So, what are we to do? We cannot abandon the developments that have brought us where we are today. After all, they do in fact sustain the community of believers. At the same time, we cannot honestly claim that they all contribute to the most effective proclamation of the Gospel. Whatever we have or do as a Church either locally or globally must be directed to proclaiming the Good News. Structures and ways of doing things, even venerable ones, are of secondary importance and must serve those ends.

We depend upon our structures and customs, but we must never lose sight of the reason for their existence. We need a sense of perspective. Jesus had such a sense. Rather than worry about other things, he devoted his ministry to proclaiming everywhere and to everyone that God's love was real and really present among them. When that proclamation required disciples, he called disciples. When it did not, he did not. The proclaiming was more important than the follow-up.

The Church that follows Jesus must be as willing to subordinate everything else to the proclamation of God's love. If that means downplaying or even abandoning certain ways of doing things, so be it. If it means not looking for institutional results, no problem.

Even if it means seeing people continue in their old religious traditions, but with a new confidence in God's love, then we must not define our mission as a search for converts. Like Jesus, we must be content to proclaim in deed and word the Good News, and call to fellowship those who are needed to further that proclamation, confident that God's love is bigger than the Church.

Fourth Sunday of the Year (A)

For Matthew, Jesus is like Moses who proclaimed God's law from Mount Sinai, and the Beatitudes are the new commandments.

So, what do the Beatitudes tell us about how we should live?

The key to them all is the first. 'How blest are the poor in spirit, the reign of God is theirs.' All the others are ways to live out this one.

To be poor in spirit is to understand my relationship with God, to understand that I have nothing to offer God that is not first of all a gift from God. Poverty of spirit frees me to accept God's greatest gift, the Kingdom, because I am not holding on to any illusions that my talents, my possessions, my time, or my life are my own.

If I am willing to settle for less than the Kingdom, allowing myself to be satisfied with the gifts rather than the Giver, I will not be able to see and accept the greater gift.

On the other hand, if I admit that before God I have nothing, I can live the Beatitudes and receive God's gifts.

'Blessed are the sorrowing; they shall be consoled.' When I admit that I cannot find comfort anywhere but in God's grace, God will comfort me. That does not mean that everything will turn out as I wish. It does mean that I will know the love of God that embraced Jesus on his cross.

'Blest are the lowly; they shall inherit the land.' Knowing my true worth before God makes me better able to know the true worth of other people. They, too, are God's gifts to the world. So, I cannot be abusive of them, or treat them as if they were mine to use as I please. Rather than 'lord it over' others, I stand with them in humility before God.

'Blest are they who hunger and thirst for holiness; they shall have their fill.' Holiness is not some other-worldly way of life. Since the birth of Jesus, the place for holiness is the real world in which I live from day to day. To be holy is to recognize in every event of my life the grace of God giving me life and love, and the call of God to share that life and love with others.

'Blest are the merciful; mercy shall be theirs.' God's love is limited only by my refusal to share it. That is the reason Jesus taught us to pray that we be forgiven to the extent that we ourselves forgive. The key to being merciful is to be honest with myself about how much I need mercy. If a sinner such as I can be forgiven, then it should be no great task to forgive others.

'Blest are the single-hearted; they shall see God.' We are not to be stubbornly single-minded, like the tortoises that Herman Melville described trying to walk through rocks: 'Their crowning curse is their drudging impulse to straightforwardness in a belittered world.' To be single-hearted means to be open to all that God offers, fully attentive at all times to the work of God in our lives. If we look for God at work, we will see God.

'Blest are the peacemakers; they shall be called children of God.' Even many Christians make the mistake of thinking that peace is merely the absence of conflict. Scripture, however, shows that peace is not an absence, but a presence. It is justice, joy, generosity, gratitude and fellowship. To be a peacemaker is to work at building those virtues in the world.

'Blest are those persecuted for holiness' sake; the reign of God is theirs. Blest are you when they insult you.' Have I ever suffered because of my Christian commitment? Not much. That is disturbing. Perhaps I do not live my faith in such a way that others even think of me as a Christian. Most of my 'persecution' is self-inflicted, a voice inside me that discourages me from living out my good intentions.

An ancient tradition of the Church is that we examine ourselves each night before going to sleep to see what sort of day we have lived. Perhaps the best way to do that is to learn and then each night repeat the Beatitudes, seeing how our day has shown us to be poor heirs of the reign of God.

Fifth Sunday of the Year (A)

Once upon a time, a researcher from a far planet visited Earth and joined a group of earthlings to learn by what means we exotic creatures take nourishment. When the group sat at table, the visitor asked about a white chemical compound that was in a vial on the table. 'Oh, that's salt,' was the answer. 'We put it on our food to improve the taste.' So, the researcher poured out a sample and swallowed it. Accusing the earthlings of being poisoners, the researcher immediately returned home in a huff with an enduring mistrust of all things terrestrial.

That night, a fisherman hauled in a fish from the deepest, darkest part of the ocean, a fish that had never seen light. The fish said to the fisherman, 'This place looks no different from my home.' The fisherman replied, 'It's dark, so it's hard to see; you need some light,' and shone a light in the fish's eyes. The dazzled denizen of the deep leapt overboard.

Hearing that the followers of Jesus are salt of the earth and light of the world would not predispose either the alienated alien or the frazzled fish to value the role of Christians in the world.

Their problem would be thinking that salt and light are themselves the focus. Salt is not something we use for its own sake; we put it on foods to improve and preserve them. Looking at a source of light is blinding. It is light reflected off of things that makes it possible for us to see them. When it comes to our use of them, salt and light do not exist for their own sakes, but for the sake of other things.

So, when Jesus tells us we are salt of the earth and light of the world, what is he saying about us? Obviously, our call to follow Christ is for the sake of the world, not our own. We are supposed to give the earth its true taste, to enable the world to see its true self.

When we look at the world, it is clear that it needs a little salt, needs some light. No one believes everything is as it should be. If the world were well salted and well lit, what would it be like? Well, certain words—'atrocity,' 'injustice,' 'poverty,' 'violence,' 'betrayal,' 'unfaithfulness,' 'falsehood' and such—would be obsolete.

Most people probably don't think it's possible to get to such a world from the one in which we live. But then, most people are not God. God seems to think it is not only possible, but possible for us.

But how can we make the whole world over? I might make me and a few others happy, but the world is a big place with big problems. Is my little bit enough to really make a difference, enough to change the world?

Look again at salt and light. They are not much in themselves. A grain of salt is pretty small. A photon, the unit of light, has zero mass. Yet, they each make a big difference.

The proverb says that 'one bad apple spoils the whole bunch.' That may be true of a crate of apples, but in today's Gospel, Jesus tells us that it does not apply to people. Good is contagious. 'Let your light shine before others, so that they may see your good works and give glory to your father in heaven.'

My bit of saltiness, my little light, can draw others to know the true taste, the true look of the world and become themselves salt and light, for to give glory to God is to be salt and light. The problem may be that the world is not getting its full ration of salt and light from us Christians. If each of us were living as Christ hopes, then the world would indeed be a different place.

So, we gather each Sunday to renew our commitment to try. By coming together, hearing the Word of God, sharing the Eucharist, singing and praying, we restore our saltiness and brighten up before going out to the world to improve its flavor. If the world is to ever become what God intends, if the kingdom for which we pray is to ever come, it will do so through the grains of salt and flickers of light we call Christians.

Sixth Sunday of the Year (A)

Jesus taught the adults and blessed the children, but the Church has gotten it backwards. That was not the case in the early days of the Church. The section of Matthew's Gospel that we call 'The Sermon on the Mount' was intended by Matthew as a sort of catechism for adults.

What Jesus says about what has been taught in the past is uncomfortably clear: those rules are not enough. His followers are allowed no anger, no abusive language, no lustful thoughts, no divorce, no oaths. It is hard to avoid the demands of these teachings. We try to water them down, claiming they apply only to certain people or are meant as ideals. It doesn't work. Jesus spoke them to the crowd, not to a specially chosen elite.

My first reaction to what Jesus says is to decide that what he wants is impossible. There is no way that I can meet his demands. So, I ignore them. But, is Jesus in fact calling upon me to do the impossible? Is the problem that he asks too much, or is it that I am unwilling to give what he asks?

When I say, 'I cannot,' do I really mean, 'I will not'? I certainly cannot say, 'I've tried to live as Christ has commanded and I know from experience that it is impossible.' As GK Chesterton remarked, 'The Christian ideal has not been tried and found wanting; it has been found difficult and left untried.'

In fact, the life Jesus calls me to has been fully lived by another. Jesus did it. It was no easier for him than for me, if what the Church teaches about his being fully human is true. He spoke from experience when he told us to go beyond the normal rules.

Those 'normal rules' are the commandments of God as taught in the Old Testament. Jesus makes the claim that God's law does not go far enough, that it is inadequate. His willingness to overrule the law of God is a sign of the divine power and authority with which Jesus taught. And that power and authority is the guarantee that somehow or other, I can, indeed, live as he calls me to do.

The reason that I can is my Baptism. In Baptism, I am united with the risen Lord, the One who has overcome death. Nothing, then, is truly impossible in living as he did. I can do it if I be willing to try.

But, how do I start? I do not have enough practice and experience to be able to easily start living according to Matthew's catechism. My fear, my weakness and my laziness are too deeply ingrained. It will take a long time to overcome them, so I must not delay.

Where do I start? Jesus talked about going beyond the usual, so perhaps the place to start is with the usual and then to go beyond it. For instance, I often limit my life of faith to part of Sunday and other spare moments during the week. So, perhaps the place to start is some day this week. Can I take time this week to live a weekday faith, for one day trying to go beyond what I consider normal? Doing so will require attention and courage. I will have to be alert to all the opportunities to live as a child of God. I will have to beware of my tendency to take the easy way.

More than anything, trying to live what Matthew presents will require prayer. I must beg the Lord for his strength, so that I may overcome the habits of a lifetime that keep me afraid or unwilling to live as he calls me to do.

It may seem as impossible as I always thought. But, it will not be impossible. The Lord does not tell us to go out and do the impossible. He does, however, command that we do nothing less than all that is possible.

That is adult faith, a faith that does not rely upon custom and rules, but goes beyond them, to a relationship with God that requires all: all my thoughts, all my talents, all my time, all my attention, all my acts.

Seventh Sunday of the Year (A)

Does God have problems? Can God have problems? It certainly appears so. Look at the evil in the world that goes counter to God's will. Look at the amount of unbelief in the world. Look at the things that believers do that give God a bad name. Look as some of the things you do. Look at what a hard time people have in trying to believe. At the very least, God has a public relations problem.

But if we grant that the Creator of the universe can have problems, what evidence is there that there might be a solution? Might we be that solution? And, even if it is possible that I am the solution or at least a solution, what must I do?

I once asked a political activist what he hoped to achieve in life. His answer was simple. 'I want to be holy.' That is what God needs of us and what God wants of us.

God tells Moses in today's first reading to give a command to the people: 'Be holy, for I, the Lord your God am holy.' That is the basic reason for all the commandments of God. The commands of God, or for that matter, of the Church, have one object, the formation of holy people.

In the gospel, Jesus tells us 'in a word, you must be perfect as your heavenly Father is perfect.' My becoming holy is obviously very important not only to me, but to God. But why?

The first reason, of course, is that God loves me and therefore wants me to grow more and more as God's image that I am meant to be. But there is another reason as well, one that touches upon God's public relations problem.

I must be perfect as God is perfect, for otherwise how will the world know how God loves?

How am I to do this? There is much I can do to show the world that God is real, that God really cares about men and women, that people can know God and become holy like God. I can be God's PR agent, loving and being holy like God and thus becoming a solution to God's problem.

What would this perfect holiness look like? Is it faultlessness? In that case, God is out of luck. I'm not able to be faultless. I'm not even sure what it would look like, since I have never met anyone else who is able to be faultless.

The same gospel passage that tells us to be perfect tells us what perfection looks like, and it is not a matter of being free of sins or defects. Neither is it some unchanging state of being. The perfection that God needs and wants from me is an activity.

It is acting like Christ in the face of his murderers, offering prayer and loving service instead of revenge. It is generosity toward those in need. It is treating all men and women as members of my family, whether they or I like it or not. That is, when you think of it, what families are all about anyway; we cannot choose our families. We can only decide to love them.

What makes other people my sisters and brothers is not a decision on my part or theirs. The choice is God's. God has chosen to be Father not only within the relationship we call Trinity, but has created, loved and redeemed us, making us children of God and therefore brothers and sisters of one another. God's choice does not depend upon whether we are good or bad. The rain falls on us all. God's choice is made out of love and we have no say in the matter.

Therefore for me to be perfect as my heavenly Father is perfect means that I must love as my Father does, without being choosy.

That's not easy. I don't know how God could manage it except that 'God is love.' But I am not love and so many of my sisters and brothers are not lovable. What can I do?

I must remember that for Catholics our highest activity is called 'Eucharist,' thanksgiving. That means that my faith is about recalling God's love for me. In return, though I cannot love as God does, in gratitude I can try. That willingness to try is perfection enough to satisfy our doting Father.

Eighth Sunday of the Year (A)

Birth, growth, work, achievement, disappointment and death—we must all go through them, but God has done so, too. God has even been ignorant with us. Jesus apparently did not know much about birds.

He says birds do not sow or reap, but almost the entire life of a bird is a search for food. The high rate at which birds use energy means that they can starve in a short time if they do not keep searching for food.

Human metabolism is slower than birds', but maintaining our health and growth requires food, water, shelter, clothing and community. We can do without some of them for a while, but the quality of our physical, emotional and even spiritual health will suffer and eventually our lives will be shortened, sometimes quite dramatically and drastically.

So, why does Jesus tell us today to not concern ourselves with such things? Does his ignorance extend to not being able to talk sensibly about human beings? Or, is he talking about an attitude toward the things we need or think we need?

'You cannot serve God and wealth.' Yet, without a certain degree of wealth, we cannot serve God. Keeping alive costs money, money we get through effort. Some people work solely for money. That is, their concern in seeking work, carrying out work, thinking about work or talking about work is money.

Some people become monsters for the sake of money. Organized crime with its drug dealing, prostitution, corruption of society and murder is one example of what some people will do for money. They destroy their own humanity and the lives of others for what they 'can't take with them.'

Others work for what money can provide. Yet, even here there are dangers. Money can be used to satisfy our basest desires, to control others, to mar the image of God in us. The First Epistle to Timothy is not kidding when it warns us that 'we brought nothing into the world, so that we can take nothing out of it; but if we have food and clothing, we will be content with these. But those who want to be rich fall into temptation and are trapped by many senseless and harmful desires that plunge people into ruin and destruction. For the love of money is a root of all kinds of evil.'

Money and the work we do to get it can bring problems, but there is a valid and healthful way to view them. The first thing is to work for the sake of the work. That does not mean living for our job; it means finding the value of our work that is not measured in terms of money. What is there about my work that makes it worth giving it my time, attention and energy? There is little work that does not have some sort of value.

Do I work for money, or in order to use God's gift of time to share in the creative eternity of God? If the latter, then the money that comes is incidental to the real reward, an interior reward. The money will sustain me and those who depend upon me, but it will not dominate me.

Considering taking a job, then, should mean more than merely looking at salary and benefits. I should try to find work that is worthy of my time and talent, work that helps build a world worthy of the sons and daughters of God. This is especially important in the case of young people.

Of course, not every situation allows people freedom to work for the sake of the value of the work. Many men, women and even children are forced into demeaning labor. Working conditions can destroy the health and lives that work should enhance. Bosses and coworkers can degrade and abuse. The pay for a worker's time and energy may not be just, not enough to sustain a dignified life.

We need food, clothing and such to survive, but we do not exist for the sake of those things or the other things money can buy. The value of work must be not solely in what we can acquire, but in our time and talent in doing it. When we work for that value, we are relying upon the gifts God has given us, and we will know that their fruits are the gift of God.

Ninth Sunday of the Year (A)

Traditionally, Christians reflect upon what are called the four last things: death, judgement, heaven and hell.

Benjamin Franklin said, 'In this world nothing can be certain, except death and taxes.' We usually use the saying only in relation to taxes. As much as we dislike them, we'd rather deal with taxes than with death.

However, the death rate really is one hundred percent. I will not escape. I will one day be extinct.

The philosopher Bertrand Russell told of a man who was asked what he thought would happen at his death. His answer was, 'Oh well, I suppose I shall inherit eternal bliss, but I wish you wouldn't talk about such unpleasant subjects.'

It is unpleasant, isn't it? The thought of not being, of decay, of perhaps winding up as an anonymous bone or two in a museum display centuries from now is no less repulsive to a believer than to an unbeliever.

Yet, my refusal to accept mortality as an integral part of God's gift of life is the underlying cause of my sin. I look for power, for possessions, for temporary satisfactions as a way of hiding from myself the fact of my temporary life. The 'cousins of death,' those failures, pains and inconveniences that remind me that I am not all-powerful, drive me to all sorts of sins and absurdities. I must reflect upon and to the extent possible accept (though we can probably never fully accept it) the reality of my death.

Nowadays, just about the only one of four last things we think about is death. But judgement seems far more important to Jesus than death. Death is not an option. We cannot control it. However, we do determine the nature of judgement. After all, God's judgement is not some abstract work; it is precisely a judgement upon what I have done and left undone in my life. I alone provide the evidence.

God takes my life seriously enough to make a statement, an absolutely honest and accurate statement, about it. That does not mean I must live in perpetual fear of God's judgement. After all, our judge is also our loving Father. However, I must not presume upon that love. I pray that I not get what I deserve, but I must not move from there to thinking that I do not deserve to be told I have betrayed God and myself in many ways throughout a lifetime.

Reflection upon judgement should influence my thoughts and deeds, not in order to bribe the judge, but so that I always recall the stakes of my life. The Lord is serious about eternity, and requires me to be so, too. Reflecting upon what I deserve from God—nothing—and remembering what I am offered—loving forgiveness—should be a daily exercise.

Judgement leads to heaven or hell. What can we say about them? Not much. Images of light, clouds, music and angels for heaven. Darkness, fire, stench, noise and demons for hell. We even present them as places, but it might be better to view afterlife as a condition rather than a place, since place is a limitation. Music, because we can neither see nor touch it yet it moves us, may be the best image we have of heaven. But even it falls short because music is of time. There simply is no way to present eternity from within time and place without using images drawn from those limited realities.

The most we can say and the least we must say about heaven is that, based upon our experience of God's love, we know it is better than we can dream of. It is the reason for our creation. We are made for heaven, and our lives should be directed toward that fulfillment of God's dreams for us.

But, we must admit that we might so totally betray those dreams, so destroy our humanity that we cannot experience heaven. Hell is a possibility. We don't know what it is. Some speak of total separation from God, others of total annihilation, the sort of death atheists believe in. Whatever it is, we must not comfort ourselves with thoughts that God loves us too much to take seriously the kind of people we make of ourselves. Jesus speaks today of the possibility of God's rejection of us. It, too, must be a motive for my life, lest I one day beyond all days hear those terrible words, 'out of my sight.'

Tenth Sunday of the Year (A)

A tax collector in the Roman Empire was not a toga-wearing version of a tax-office bureaucrat. First and foremost, he was a traitor to his own people, working on behalf of the foreign conquerors.

Not only was Matthew a traitor, he was a gouger as well. A tax collector bought the job, and was entitled to grab as much as he could to get his money back and then some. It's little wonder that decent folks avoided tax collectors.

It's also little wonder that when Jesus went to Matthew's home for dinner decent folk took note and commented. Since Jesus was a teacher, his meals were supposed to be symbols of the joyous gathering of the saved in the Kingdom of God. If he was willing to sit and eat with Matthew and 'many tax collectors and those known to be sinners,' Jesus was saying something about the Kingdom, something the good people did not want to hear. He was saying that God accepts such sinners and expects the good people to share heaven with them.

The Pharisees did not like to be told that they might have to share the Kingdom with people with whom they would rather not share the planet. Am I really all that different? Indeed, 'good Christian men and women' are often no better than good Pharisee men and women, even though we are supposed to know better.

We share the Eucharist, the foretaste of the eschatological banquet, with all sorts of men and women all over the world, yet we exclude some of those same people from our care, our concern, our service and our love. Heaven is going to be an embarrassing place for many of us, especially if there is assigned seating.

I wouldn't mind being with some of the people who repel me if they were to change. After all, doesn't the Church preach repentance?

Sinners and other unsavory characters should change, and then they are welcome to my world.

However, Jesus seems to have gotten things backwards. He did not tell Matthew to repent and then follow. He did not tell Matthew's friends to repent at the door before coming to the table. He shared the table, a taste of heaven, with them without conditions. Apparently, he felt that repentance is easier for those who know they are already loved than it is for those who have to buy love with repentance.

At a soup kitchen in Japan I overheard one of the guests asking the one next to him, 'Why do these people do this for us?' The answer was gratifying and challenging: 'They're Christians; they care about people like us.'

Do we? Do I? Had those same two men showed up at my house, would they have been welcomed? What if they had approached me on the street? Would I share a meal with them? Had they come to a church, would we welcome them? Share the Eucharist with them?

We usually don't even share the Eucharist with non-Catholic Christians. We say that we ourselves must be 'in a state of grace' to share it. Sinners may be welcome at the table of the Kingdom, but not at the table of the Kingdom's servant, the Church. Does that mean that I should welcome any and all to the Eucharist? Perhaps it does, but since it is not my Eucharist, but the Church's, I probably do not have that right. Sometimes being a member of a community means being part of the community's sin.

Be that as it may, there are many parts of my life where I cannot blame the Church or society for my failure to welcome every man and woman as a brother or sister with whom I will spend eternity. My willingness to befriend and serve them will become for some of them the medicine they need to be healed of the weaknesses and sins that repel me. If I can think of their needs rather than my repulsion (or, more often, my reputation and comfort), the very thing that repels me may find healing.

Self-righteousness is not only an ugly sin, it is a foolish one. After all, who am I to decide that others' sins put them beyond the pale? Perhaps self-righteousness, choosiness about with whom we will sit, is the one sin that will keep us outside the banquet hall.

Eleventh Sunday of the Year (A)

'When Jesus saw the crowds, he had compassion for them, because they were harassed and helpless, like sheep without a shepherd.' It is easy to imagine such a crowd. We have all seen images of refugees fleeing violence or starvation. Their drooping shoulders, shuffling gait, sunken eyes and ragged clothes define for us what it means to be 'harassed and helpless.'

That 'definition,' however, is too narrow. Jesus was moved to pity not by encountering an extraordinary situation of suffering, but as he 'went about all the cities and villages.' The harassed and helpless sheep whom he saw were the people he met on the streets of those cities and villages.

Seen through the eyes and with the heart of Jesus, the world of the harassed and helpless is not some far-off place. It is my home, my community. Sheep without a shepherd are all around me. I am often one myself.

What is life like for a shepherdless sheep? Shepherds provide protection from predators when that is needed, but their major task is simply to provide guidance for the sheep, protecting them from the exhausting futility of aimless wandering.

Are the people around me aimless wanderers? If I were to ask them on a street corner as they wait impatiently for the signal that will allow them to cross the busy street, they would deny being aimless. They would say they know exactly where they want to go or have to go and they know how to get there.

A certain job, the right deal, useful contacts, good health, hard work, a little bit of luck and a bit more time will get them where they want to be. However, if pressed, they have a hard time saying exactly where that is. 'Success,' 'happiness,' 'wealth,' 'a sense of being useful'—all these and more might be their answers. But, what do they mean?

Can I really say forthrightly what my life is heading toward? Am I satisfied that there are no doubts about it? Can I honestly say that I and those around me are not harassed and helpless in the face of life? Of course not.

So, I can place myself and those I know among those whom Jesus looked upon as being like sheep without a shepherd. We are the ones he looks upon with compassion.

So, then what? What does Jesus do for us? In the gospel passage, he calls upon his disciples to pray that workers be sent among the lost wanderers so that they may be drawn to God like a harvest.

However, prayer in the abstract is not enough. It will not do to pray that God take care of the problems of the world without being willing to be the means God uses to do that. So, the next thing Jesus does is to give a new commission those whom he told to pray.

The disciples whom he chose are named, but the names are not important. In fact, we do not know for sure the names of all of the Twelve. The Gospels do not agree on the list. That does not matter. Jesus picked them not because of who they were, but because of the vocation he offered them. Any Tom, Dick or Harry would do. Apparently, even you and I will do. In fact, if we obey Jesus' command to 'ask the Lord of the harvest to send out laborers into his harvest' we should expect to be chosen to be those laborers.

We are chosen to go to the 'lost sheep' and tell them the Good News that 'the kingdom of heaven has drawn near.' The evidence that we give for the truth of our message is our work to heal the sick, to restore the outcast, to relieve physical, mental and spiritual suffering and our offer of this service and Good News to all without seeking return for ourselves.

My life as a Christian is not some sort of fortuitous accident. I have been chosen by God just as the Twelve were chosen. I have been sent as they were sent. Somewhere in this world there is someone for whom I am God's gift.

Twelfth Sunday of the Year (A)

We have probably always have had and probably always will have a fascination with the eerily alien—ghosts, demons, monsters, ogres, wraiths, witches, space invaders and the rest of their ilk. Some people's attitudes toward angels, saints and even God probably also fit into this phenomenon.

Modern science, rather than dispelling such ideas, merely gives them new garb. The great-great grandchildren of those who dwelt at the edge of the forest and heard spooks in the rustling trees now fly airplanes and search the skies for UFOs.

Our ghosts, ghouls and goblins share a common characteristic: they are usually threatening. They are the stuff of nightmares. We do not want to meet them, and merely to hear about them or see them on a TV, movie or computer screen is frightening. Frightening, yet fascinating.

In fact, we seem obsessed with monsters. From children's cartoons to pseudo-scientific seminars on alien abductors, we are drawn again and again to considering the possibility of some non-human, anti-human presences lurking in the shadows, ready to destroy us. Some say they are inventions of our minds to help us come to grips with the reality of death. Since in our stories the hero or heroine (in other words, myself in some guise) always wins, we are winning over death.

'Do not fear those who kill the body but cannot kill the soul; rather fear him who can destroy both body and soul in hell,' says Jesus in today's Gospel passage from Matthew.

With this admonition, Jesus gives us the answer to dealing with ghosts, aliens and whatever else comes along, including certain fellow human beings. His advice even applies to accidents and natural events like storms, earthquakes, disease and wild animals as well as any other form of danger to my life: Do not be afraid.

Why not? Even if some of our fears are directed toward fictions like visitors from other planets, some fears are based in reality. Isn't Jesus being unrealistic to tell us not to fear?

The answer comes in the rest of what he says in the Gospel. 'Do not be afraid; you are of more value than many sparrows.' In fact, nowadays in Tokyo grilled sparrows cost somewhat less than a bowl of noodles. So, is our worth, while more than that of the sparrows, lower than, say, that of a meal in a good restaurant?

Of all my boyhood toys, the one I best remember was not really a toy at all. It was a broken radiator exhaust valve. It was worth nothing in the marketplace, but with just a little imagination it could be so many things. I valued it immeasurably. Though it is now probably buried in a landfill somewhere or was long ago melted as scrap, it remains a treasure in my memory. Worth and value are two different measures, and Jesus is dealing with value rather than worth.

Our value of which Jesus speaks is not something that we have in ourselves, our market worth. Our value is given to us by God, and it is an inflated value, far beyond what we are actually worth. In fact, it is infinite, because its measure is the infinite love of God.

That is the reason the Psalm says we need not 'fear the terror of the night, or the arrow that flies by day, or the pestilence that stalks in the darkness, or the destruction that wastes at noonday.'

God is in love with us, and therefore we need not fear the real or imagined threats around us. There are terrors in our lives, but measured against the love and power of God, they are nothing. As the Church's Sunday Night Prayer says, 'Night holds no terror for me sleeping under God's wing.'

And so, we go to the housetops to proclaim that love. In a world full of terrors, we have been commissioned to share the Good News that we need not fear. God's love protects us. God's love embraces us eternally, overcoming fear, overcoming death.

Thirteenth Sunday of the Year (A)

The fourth-century patriarch of Constantinople, Saint John Chrysostom, commenting on the wealth he saw on the altar and in the church around him, gave a sermon that makes reference to something Jesus says today.

'Do you wish to honor the Body of Christ? Do not despise him when he is naked. Do not honor him here in the church building with silks, only to neglect him outside, where he is suffering from cold and from nakedness . . . Of what use is it to load the table of Christ? Feed the hungry and then come and decorate the table. You are making a golden chalice and do not give a cup of cold water? The Temple of your afflicted brother's body is more precious than this Temple (the church).'

Jesus said, 'whoever gives even a cup of cold water to one of these little ones in the name of a disciple—truly I tell you, none of these will lose their reward.'

In Matthew's Gospel, 'little ones' are the disciples whom Jesus has sent into the world to share the Good News. So, as we go about our daily lives trying to show others the difference that Christ has made in our lives, their response to us is a response to Jesus and they will be rewarded. We are an opportunity for blessing for those whom we meet.

However, Chrysostom touches on a point that we should consider today because it is one of the great obstacles to our being a source of blessing to the world. If people do not perceive something of Christ in us, we are not being true disciples of Christ. If we have not taken up the cross to follow Christ, how will our brothers and sisters see him today?

When people see us, what do they see? A community of people who love Christ more than anyone or anything else? Men and women who are willing to give their lives for his sake and as he did for the sake of the world? In other words, do they see Christ in his Church, the Body of Christ?

Yes and no.

Perhaps they see the beautiful churches we have erected to the glory of God. Perhaps, too, they see the poor at the doors of those churches, hoping that Christians won't drive them away from sleeping on the steps.

Perhaps they see our institutions of healing and learning. Perhaps they also see men and women who cannot have access to those institutions because they cannot afford their services.

Perhaps they see our organizations that collect vast sums to assist the poor throughout the world. Perhaps they also see that much of that wealth is produced by economic and social systems that glorify possession over generosity, selfishness over sharing. Perhaps they see us calculating how little we need give to salve our consciences, but not factoring in the pained needs of the world.

Perhaps they see our voluntary acts of service to the world. Perhaps they also see our selfishness, our complacency, our cruelty.

Perhaps they read and are moved by our Scriptures that speak of God's love for all of us. Perhaps, too, they see how little we allow that word to shape our lives.

Perhaps they hear our prayers, sermons and hymns and sense in them the voice of God. Perhaps, too, they hear the backbiting, the slander and the viciousness of so much that Christians say even about each other.

Perhaps some of them even see me.

Part of the call of Christ is a call to repentance. It is not something I can reserve to Lent or an occasional confession. Because nearly my whole life is a nay-saying to God, my whole life must be repentance.

I must beg God for the grace and courage to say in deeds the 'Yes' I said in Baptism when Christ called me to take up his cross and follow him.

In fact, the grace and courage are always offered. When I am ready to accept them, perhaps then I will truly become one among the prophets and little ones who will draw the world to Christ.

Fourteenth Sunday of the Year (A)

What if I were to say, 'learn from me, for I am humble'?

The problem would be that I myself could not believe what I was saying. I would know that anything I said about my own humility would be a form of bragging. I might do it with the most subdued tone and downcast eyes, but my message would still be, 'Hey! Look at me—I'm being humble!'

I know my weakness, my fears, my stupidity, my stubbornness, my ignorance and my laziness are too much a part of me to leave much room for anything about which I can brag. I have plenty of reasons to be humble.

If I tried to brag about anything, least of all humility, those who love me would laugh; others would sneer. Both would be correct.

But, Jesus could get away with it. Why do we let him claim to be humble when we know how hollow our own claims to humility are?

It is important to see the context of Jesus' claim to humility. When I claim to be humble either to others or to myself, I am thinking about myself. When Jesus spoke about being humble, he was talking about others.

'Come to me, all you that are weary and are carrying heavy burdens, and I will give you rest.'

The humility of Jesus is an element in his service to others. He presents his humility as evidence that they can trust him to care for them. They can take his yoke upon themselves, knowing that he will make it an easy load.

We sometimes seem to think of humility as a way of speaking—in subdued, self-deprecating tones, or even as a cringing posture. Jesus shows us today that humility is neither words nor appearances, but a quality that shows itself in deeds.

Humility is the quality in us that enables others to trust that we will help them bear the burdens of life. People will know they can trust me to help them because I actually help them without thought of inconvenience to me.

We sometimes confuse humility and shyness. Shyness makes me want to be invisible. However, humility requires being noticed. How can others know they can trust my service if they never see my service? However, what is done is more important than who does it. It is my service that they should note, not me. I should be humbly noticeable and noticeably humble, drawing attention to the work of God who uses me as an instrument.

So, if I wish to be able to say with Jesus that I am humble, I must shut up and get to work. There is no shortage of people in my world who are heavily burdened. They are lonely, they are sick, they are hopeless and unaware of the love that God has for them.

Why should I worry about their burdens when I have enough of my own? The Nobel Peace Prize-winning organist, theologian and medical missionary Albert Schweitzer once told a group of young people, 'I don't know what your destiny will be, but one thing I know. The only ones among you who will be really happy are those who have sought and found how to serve.'

If I hope to share the kind of joyful closeness to the Father that Jesus shows in the prayer that opens today's reading, there is no other way than the way of humble service. I must put the needs of others before my own. When I do so, another's burden is eased, but I, too, benefit from finding a new peace of heart that eases my own burdens.

When I can be humble in this way, then the words of Jesus apply to me. 'All things have been handed over to me by my Father; and no one knows the Son except the Father, and no one knows the Father except the Son and anyone to whom the Son chooses to reveal him.'

When I imitate the serviceable humility of Jesus, I come to know God in a new way, the way of Jesus. The world around me may be in turmoil, but I will be in peace and calm, not because I am apart from the world, but because I am sharing God's deep love for that world.

Fifteenth Sunday of the Year (A)

There were three stages in the formation of the Gospels. The first was the life of Jesus himself and what he said and did.

The second stage was the period of proclamation of Jesus after the Resurrection, when the presentation was adapted to the missionary needs of the preachers. They combined sayings, arranging them in an effective order for teaching purposes.

The third was the actual writing of the Gospel accounts, writing influenced by the experience and needs of the particular communities for which the Gospels were written.

The Parable of the Sower shows this sort of development. We have a parable of Jesus, an explanation of parables in general and then an interpretation that is presented as his, but which actually comes out of the experience of the later Church. Both the original intent of the parable and the interpretation bear important messages for us today.

The sower in the parable broadcasts the seeds rather than planting them one by one. The ground was plowed and then the seed was sown. Since the weeds in the field were plowed under rather than removed, weeds sprang up along with the crop.

Since the seed was simply thrown around, it could land just about anywhere, including on the paths that had been packed down by generations of people walking them.

What is Jesus talking about? This parable begins a section of Matthew's Gospel that deals with the growth of the Reign of God. That Reign always looks unpromising, but God works in ways that we cannot see to bring it to fruition.

No matter where some of the seed may land and the odds against it, the growth of the Reign of God is unstoppable.

That's the seed, but what of the sower?

The sower is anyone chosen to spread the Good News of the Reign of God. In other words, the sower is anyone who is a follower of Christ. You or me.

But, am I really a sower? I doubt it. I am willing to speak of my faith and live my faith, but usually in certain limited circumstances. There are probably people with whom I work or among whom I live who have little or no idea that I am a disciple of Christ. Even if they know that I carry a Christian label, they may not know what my faith means to me.

'When the time is right.' 'When they bring up the subject.' 'When it won't matter what they think of me.' Not for me the sower throwing seeds on paths, in weed patches, on stones or on fertile soil—anywhere and everywhere.

In other words, I do not broadcast the seeds of faith, entrusting the harvest to God. There is too little about my deeds and words that would give anyone else any idea, or even remind myself, what it means to be a Christian.

It is here that the interpretation Matthew gave the parable becomes important for my life. God will bring the harvest to fruition, but sowers are needed. In other words, God needs me to be a person in whom the Word has borne fruit.

I am one who hears the Word without understanding it. It is not that the Word is difficult to comprehend. The problem is that I do not pay attention. Even paying attention to the Word as read in the liturgy appears beyond me. I seldom go looking for the Word in Scripture or in the events of my day.

I am one who receives the Word with joy, but I fail to persevere in it because I fail to reflect upon that Word in prayer and meditation. That sort of 'faith' is unready to follow Christ to the cross.

I am one who hears the Word, but I am too busy. I have other priorities and responsibilities. Isn't it enough to say I am a Christian, go to church and leave it at that?

But, I am at times also one who hears the Word and allows it to sink roots into my heart. When I do that, my life bears fruit.

Which kind of hearer will I be today? How will I receive the Word today, right now? Am I willing to commit myself for this week, or at least today, to be one who sows the Word in word and deed? Will I live in such a way that could at least give others the suspicion that I might be a Christian?

Sixteenth Sunday of the Year (A)

Jesus talks of a field where wheat and the weed darnel are growing. Darnel resembles wheat, so it is hard to go into a field of closely growing grass and separate it from wheat. Even if you can tell the difference, the roots are so intertwined that pulling up one plant will destroy several others.

When the evangelist put this parable into his Gospel, he aimed it at an experience the Church faced in the first century and still faces twenty centuries later. Weeds.

We are the crop of Christ, sown in the world to show the love of God. But, something has gone wrong. There are weeds in the field. They look like wheat, like the true harvest of saints, and sometimes it is hard to tell one from the other, but weeds are among us.

One need not be an expert in the Church's history or current events to know that we are a very mixed crop. There is not a single sin from which we Christians are exempt. We've committed them all and might even be responsible for inventing a few new ones.

There are some weeds that fool me into thinking they are healthy fruit bearers. I have no problem pointing out some of the more obvious weeds in the Church.

Christ went to the cross for me, but he is not getting his crucifixion's worth out of me, that's for sure. I am, too often, one of the weeds in his Church.

My problem is that I am a sort of hybrid. The Lord sowed me as good seed for the growth of his Gospel. But, there is some degree of weed in me. Not only does his field, the Church, contain weeds; even the wheat is a bit weedy.

Which way will I go? I can become weedier; that's for sure. Can I become grainier? Am I tending toward one or the other today? Am I a seed for the growth of the Kingdom of God?

Fortunately, God's Reign does not depend totally upon me. It does not even depend totally upon the whole Church. God will make it happen. Even small, hybrid seed like me can somehow bear fruit because God will make us do so. Mustard seed is not actually the smallest seed and the mustard plant is only a moderately large shrub, but the bush it becomes is much greater than one would expect from looking at the seed.

So, I have reason to hope that the good in me will not be totally overwhelmed by the weedy and will be of some use to God in making the Kingdom come. My little bit will serve, like a bit of yeast, to bring the whole world to God.

How can I cooperate in this? How can I nurture the mustard seed of God in me, how can I be leaven for the world, when I know that I am so weedy?

I cannot do it on my own. Just as the Kingdom will be brought about through God's power, so, too, will my part in building that Kingdom be brought about through God's power. I need only prepare myself for that power to work in me.

But how?

St Paul tells the Christians in Rome that he faces the same problem. Our weakness is too strong for us to overcome it. But, Paul tells us that 'the Spirit helps us in our weakness.'

We gather on Sunday in order, among other things, to pray that the Kingdom come. Prayer is the operation that allows the good in us to overcome the evil. It is the means by which we hybrids can become more and more like good seed.

In our prayer, God makes the seemingly impossible happen. The seed of good flourishes, the world is leavened. All we need do is pray.

But how?

No matter how much God may be satisfied with my prayer, I am not. I want it to be deeper, more fervent, more frequent and more 'effective' than it actually is. That is because I look upon it as something that I do.

But, Paul tells me not to worry, because 'we do not know how to pray as we ought, but that very Spirit intercedes with sighs too deep for words.' If I wish to pray to be better seed, the Spirit of God will do that praying for me. And then, little hybrid though I may be, I will take my place in the field of the Lord, being good grain for the world.

Seventeenth Sunday of the Year (A)

Jesus describes something that happens all over the world. The ground can be a handy storage place for treasure, especially in times of invasion or unrest. Since those who do the burying often do not return to reclaim their hoard, it remains in the ground to be discovered later by archaeologists, treasure hunters, house builders and farmers.

We are unlikely to find buried treasure in a field and then sell all we have to buy it. We might be more likely to hear a good stock tip or racing tip and invest all we have in that. The circumstances differ, but the response is the same. When we have the chance to acquire a treasure at a bargain rate, we want it.

Is the Reign of God a bargain? Jesus seems to think so. Using all we have to get it is worth the cost.

Yet, most of the world's people do not seem to think the bargain worth the cost. Christians are a minority. For that matter, though I am a Christian, I am not sure that I am willing to make a big investment. Why do people not respond to a great offer that includes knowing the love of God that gives us life beyond death?

If some scruffy-looking character were to walk up to me and say, 'I have a great investment for you. All you have to do is take my word for it and hand over all you have,' what would I do?

That may be part of the reason the world has not taken up the bargain offered by Jesus. Look at his agents—the Church. We have our glories, but they are often obscured by other things.

That is not merely true of the Church as an institution. Look at the Christians you know. Look at yourself. As the saying goes, 'Would you buy a used car from this person?' What if the asking price were all one had?

There is a legitimate 'scruffiness' in the Church. The Cross does not look like victory. However, it is seldom the scandal of the Cross that keeps people from buying into the Kingdom of God. It is usually the scandal of Christians that does so.

I think the problem is that we Christians have not really 'bought' the Good News of the Kingdom ourselves.

I am a Christian by habit, not by single-hearted desire. When I look at the amount of energy and dedication people put into worldly pursuits—most of them quite legitimate—health, prosperity, career, education, family, relaxation etc, and compare the amount of time and energy I put into being a Christian, I am embarrassed.

If I will not deepen my knowledge of and love for Scripture, if prayer is something I do mechanically if at all, if my service to others is grudging, if my worship is wooden formality, how can I be a convincing purveyor of the treasure of God? If I obviously have not made an investment in it, why should anyone else?

The Kingdom of God is like a dragnet. Everyone who comes into contact with it is drawn in, but the fish who are caught are sent not to the chowder pot, but back to the nets, this time as fishers. Since the whole world must be caught, even the fish must help catch. The life of the Kingdom of God in this world is missionary.

Our vocation is to be bait for the Kingdom. Our lives must arouse curiosity, attraction and, finally, commitment on the part of those to whom God sends us. And God sends us to everyone.

However, if we have repelled others, if our hypocrisy makes the Gospel message of the Kingdom repulsive to them, then we will be judged useless and be thrown away.

How can I become like some learned scribe who can speak with confident knowledge of the Reign of God? St Paul tells me that if I love God, then all that I do and all that happens to me will somehow work toward the building of God's Reign. I may not do everything well, but God's love will bring about its fruition.

My love for God comes from knowing God loves and calls me. I have been 'predestined to be conformed to the image of his Son.' Just as Jesus was sent to be the sign of the coming Reign of God, I am sent. Can there be a greater vocation than that?

We are other Christs for the world. Let's get out today and help the world find and buy that treasure.

Eighteenth Sunday of the Year (A)

God is a great disappointment, the ultimate underachiever. There are probably more people who think this way than there are actual atheists in the world. Believers who are honest some time or other face the problem that God does not seem to be measuring up to the job.

Look at the evidence. Each year, tens of thousands die because they do not get enough food. Even more are so weakened that they are not able to live with any semblance of the dignity that belongs to those made in the image of God.

Diseases that we once thought defeated are once again becoming epidemic and a new one, AIDS, is destroying whole societies in Africa and Southeast Asia as well as bringing suffering and early death to many in other parts of the world.

Millions of people are refugees, driven by poverty and violence from their homes. Injustice is rampant. Natural disasters occur again and again.

Closer to home, my life is not as I wish. Friendships end, plans fail, selfishness and laziness overwhelm hopes and dreams. I sin, I fail. I die.

Atheists have chosen the easy answer—they do not have to face the difficult facts of life while holding a faith that says there is a God and that God is love. Believers have the harder task of admitting that God does not meet the standards we set.

Yet, many of those who suffer the failures of God continue to believe. We seem more willing to accept lower performance from God than nonbelievers are willing to do. The reason may be that we somehow realize that God's performance is actually better than we give credit for.

In Exodus, God tells Moses to tell the people, 'The Lord, the God of your fathers, the God of Abraham, Isaac and Jacob, has appeared to me and said: "I am concerned about you."'

Is that it? God is concerned? Is that enough? Even if it were enough to satisfy God, would it satisfy me? No.

'When Jesus went ashore, he saw a great crowd and he had compassion for them and cured their sick.' The compassion of Jesus is proof that God is not insensitive to the pains and needs of the world. God feels for us, but does more. Jesus heals, God uses Moses to lead the Hebrews to freedom.

But, that was long ago and far away. What about today? If God feels compassion today, what does God do about it?

The disciples come to Jesus and tell him the people are hungry. They are not unlike us when we pray, telling God to fill the hungers of the world.

Jesus gives a clear answer to them and to us: '*You* give them something to eat.'

Jesus has given us the task of answering the prayers of the world. Can it be that the problems of the world could actually be solved by us, the disciples of Christ? It certainly looks impossible, as impossible as feeding more than five thousand people with five loaves and two fish.

It has certainly not worked. Of course, perhaps it has not really been tried yet. When Jesus fed the crowd, there were twelve baskets of food left over. In other words, each of the apostles worked, carrying a basket. Could it be that we are hoping that someone else—God, for instance—will do the task that requires every set of Christian hands?

What would happen if we were to take seriously God's willingness to do the impossible through disciples? Am I willing to take the risk today to find out?

The feeding of the crowd is the only miracle of Jesus to appear in all four Gospels. It apparently contains a message for us that no account of the life and teaching of Jesus could be without.

The Gospels present it in terms of the Eucharist. Taking bread, blessing it, breaking it and sharing it are the four elements that describe the action of Jesus and his Church in our most important activity.

However, in all four Gospels, the Eucharist is linked to the responsibility of the disciples to feed the multitude. Can bread be the Body of Christ? We declare that it can be his real presence among us. Can we say that it is any less likely that God will work through you and me?

God is not shirking. The answer to the prayers of the world has been given. We are that answer. Who, then, is the disappointing underachiever, God who has provided the answer, or we, the answer provided?

Nineteenth Sunday of the Year (A)

One of my favorite childhood books was *The Little Engine That Could*, about a small locomotive that goes up a hill that larger engines have failed to climb. The little engine was able to do so because it said over and over, 'I think I can, I think I can, I think I can.' Because it thought it could, it in fact became the little engine that could.

I loved *The Little Engine That Could* because it gave me confidence. That is probably the reason the story was told in the first place—as a way to encourage children facing the big, confusing, grown-up-dominated world.

That may be part of the reason the story of Peter on the water is in Matthew's Gospel. The evangelist wanted to encourage the Church and individual Christians to trust in the power of the Lord.

Peter's walking on water was not Jesus' idea. It was Peter's: 'Lord, if it is you, command me to come to you across the water.' It is a rather peculiar request—'Tell me to do the impossible.'

So, Jesus tells him to go ahead and do the impossible: 'Come.'

And Peter does. He walks on water. Perhaps as he got out of the boat and stepped onto the water, he was thinking, 'I think I can, I think I can, I think I can.'

So long as he thought so, he could and did walk on the water.

The problem came because 'when he noticed the strong wind, he became frightened.' His 'I think I can' became a sensible 'I can't do this!' So, he started sinking and cried to the Lord to save him.

Jesus did so, but at the same time he scolded Peter. 'You of little faith, why did you doubt?'

But, why should Peter not doubt? After all, people do not walk on water. One should not even try something so unrealistic.

We are like Peter. We ask the Lord to have us do the impossible—to bring peace and justice, to forgive, to show the love of God to the world—and he says, 'Go ahead!'

How realistic is that? History, reason and our hearts tell us it is impossible. What cause have we to think that we can do the impossible?

But, what is impossible? It is impossible for a little engine to climb a big hill. It is impossible for a Galilean fisherman to walk on water.

The writer Arthur C Clarke said, 'If an elderly but distinguished scientist says that something is possible he is almost certainly right, but if he says that it is impossible, he is very probably wrong.'

Clarke's comment is certainly true of other realms as well as of science. We decide ahead of time what is impossible and then fail to do what is actually possible.

And yet, we have imitated Peter in asking the Lord to give us an 'impossible' task. By accepting the title 'Christian' we say that we are willing, even anxious, to do the impossible.

Of course, Peter did not walk on water through his own power even if it was his own idea. It was Jesus responding to Peter's faith that kept him up. Peter's thought may have actually been, 'I think he can, I think he can, I think he can.'

Committing himself to Jesus enabled Peter not only to suggest and accept the Lord's call to come across the water, but to actually do so. When his faith faltered, he foundered.

The Lord is willing to support us in doing the impossible. What we need is enough faith to enable us to step out of the security of the boat we call everyday 'sensible' life. To love the world as God loves it, we need foolhardy courage.

Peter starts his request by saying, 'Lord, if it is you.' If Jesus is the Lord, the presence of God among us, then we, like Peter, should clamor to do the impossible.

Does the world see the with resentment and bitterness? 'Command me to forgive.'

Does the world suffer injustice? 'Command me to be a peacemaker.'

Does the world stagger under the weight of hopelessness? 'Command me to preach the Gospel.'

All I need is confidence that Jesus is indeed the Son of God.

Then, my motto becomes, 'I think I can because I know he can,' and the world will see me do the impossible. I will be The Little Christian That Could.

Twentieth Sunday of the Year (A)

More than the other evangelists, Matthew looks to the Old Testament. That may be why he used the ancient designation, Canaanite, for someone from a place no longer called Canaan.

In the Old Testament, Canaanites are the prime example of godless evil. By calling the woman a Canaanite, Matthew is emphasizing her otherness, her probable sinfulness and her total difference from Jews.

It is a difference that Jesus responded to in a typical way. Typical, that is, for his society. He abused her. She was a foreigner and a pagan. Any Jew would have been curt with her. Jesus did not even bother to answer her.

How can that be? How could he have been so cold-hearted toward a woman seeking help for her tortured daughter? The most likely answer was that he was raised that way.

We are all shaped by the society in which we grow up. Usually, we do not change unless something happens that makes us look at our prejudices in a new way. Travel, learning another language, reading literature, studying history or living in another culture can give us opportunities to view ourselves and the world from new perspectives.

The Incarnation means that Jesus really was a man of his time, his place and his people. He spoke their language, he dressed as they dressed, he had the same prejudices they had. But, he was willing to learn. That is what happened when he met the foreign woman.

Apparently Jesus did not see himself as having a mission to those outside Israel. That is one reason that the move toward the Gentiles by the early Church provoked controversy. Some Christians wondered why the Church should do what Jesus had not done. It was probably as a response to that attitude that Matthew included the story of Jesus's meeting with the woman in the gospel.

So, what happens in the story? The conversion of Jesus. When he tells the woman that his ministry is not for dogs like her, she betters him in the repartee.

Failing to find a good retort, Jesus admits defeat not only in the interchange, but the defeat of his prejudice as well. He saw faith where he did not expect to find it and learned from the woman that his mission was not bounded by the limitations of his society and human background.

Was Jesus changed merely because he met a woman who was wittier than he? No, the woman's victory did not come from having a quick tongue. She was willing to approach Jesus, a foreigner whose religion differed from hers. Perhaps she wondered if her gods or her neighbors might be offended by that. She endured his silence and persisted in her request. She used her wits in arguing with him.

Where did she get that desperate courage and strength? Her strength was in her love for her child. For the sake of her daughter, she would endure ridicule and rejection without giving up. Jesus, the love of God, could only respond positively to that.

What about me? When I make decisions, do I listen for 'wisdom,' for 'rationality,' for 'common sense,' for 'what's in it for me?' Do I listen to the prejudices of my time and place?

Or do I listen for love? When I hear politicians and leaders do I try to find love, especially love of the powerless, in what they say and do? When teachers, neighbors, family, friends, strangers or organizations make requests or suggestions to me, do I listen for the voices of love? Do I listen when love speaks in my own heart, or do I deafen myself to that voice?

Sometimes I will not find love in what I hear and see. I may find selfishness or stupidity. Sometimes my own self-interest and prejudice blind me to the real message. When Jesus merely listened to the request of that alien woman, he missed the point. When she made him hear her love, he grew. Seeing her love, he did what his own great love demanded and he healed the girl.

I must listen to all who love, even though they differ from me. They may be the voice of wisdom, calling me to understand and show God's love better. I must be willing to listen and look where I might rather not. The voices of love are calls to conversion to God who is love. When I have been converted, then I will do as Jesus did, being a better sign of the good news of God's love for the whole world.

Twenty-First Sunday of the Year (A)

Shakespeare may not have thought much of Jesus' calling his chief disciple 'Rock.' In *Julius Caesar* Marullus berates the people of Rome: 'You blocks, you stones, you worse than senseless things!'

That's one way of looking at Simon's nickname. By calling him Peter (Rock), is Jesus saying that the man is 'as sharp as a bowling ball'? The Gospels do not portray Peter as the brightest of the disciples.

The old 'Rocky' movies give another possibility for understanding Peter's nickname. Is Simon the strong man who will overcome, though all the odds are against him? Swinging his sword at Gethsemane certainly shows that he was ready for a brawl.

Might Simon be rock-like in stubbornness, unwilling or unable to be moved by argument or common sense? That might be, though Saint Paul once 'opposed him to his face' for being wishy-washy.

Or, might Jesus have called him Rock because he was dependable, committed, steady in the face of opposition? But then, there was that shameful business of denying Jesus during his trial.

Another possibility is that Simon was seen by Jesus as strong enough to provide support for others, a rock-solid foundation. That is certainly implied in what Jesus says after the naming: 'on this rock I will build my church.'

The Gospel says that Jesus chose to build his Church on Peter the Rock. Did Jesus decide to do so because of Peter's rock-ness? Might it not be the other way around? Is the Church built on Peter because he is the Rock, or is he the Rock because the Lord chose to build the Church on him?

The answer is important for us, because in a sense the Church is built upon each of us. So, must we be rock-like in order to be good Christians?

If to be a Christian requires that I be a rock, there are, indeed, some ways in which the description fits.

Certainly, we can be capable of gross stupidity—blocks, stones, and worse than senseless things. Yet, like Peter, we are capable also of being the recipients of God's inspiration.

We can be like Simon Peter in being rambunctious, ready to rush off on behalf of the Lord, but disappointed and fearful when the battle against our own sin and the sin of the world gets to be difficult.

On the other hand, we can be stubborn in holding to the customs of faith, but too willing to compromise with the world when it comes to the actual living of that faith.

Am I rocklike in steadiness? Well, sort of. But, I worry too much about 'fitting in.' My friendships, my position in society, even my livelihood depend upon not being too different, especially in the ways that faith calls me to be different.

A rock of support, then? Sometimes. But, I prefer to support others at my convenience rather than at their need. I have commitments of my own that are more important to me.

Perhaps most appropriate would be the image of 'rock bottom,' as low as one can go. All in all, neither I nor my fellow Christians are all that impressive.

If Jesus had nicknamed Simon 'Gelatin,' that might have been more accurate not only of him, but also of us, the Church built upon him as foundation—somewhat firm, but wobbly.

Is it sufficient to be gelatin rather than rock? The Lord seems to think so. In the case of Simon Peter, Christ's decision to build the Church upon him turned him into a rock foundation. Simon who denied the Lord, Simon who ran away at the final test of the Cross, became Peter, the leader of the disciples and martyr for Christ.

The key to Simon's shift from gelatin to rock is his admission that Jesus is 'the Messiah, the Son of the living God.' That admission did not turn him into rock, but it was all Jesus needed to declare that he would suffice as a foundation.

Is my weak faith gelatinous enough for Jesus to declare the same of me? It probably is. I say that Jesus is the Lord, and he makes me a foundation for the building up of the Church.

Does that mean I will never again waver, quaver? Of course not. Peter shook many times even after being renamed Rock.

The important thing about Peter and the important thing about me is that Christ has chosen us to be Church. He has set us up in all our weakness and declared that the gates of death will not prevail against us.

Twenty-Second Sunday of the Year (A)

There is no Christian life without the cross. Yet, we do not want it. As a decoration, it looks nice. As the searing torture of body, mind and spirit that it really is, we want no part of it.

Peter was not the last follower of Jesus who has felt, 'God forbid it, Lord! This must never happen to you—or me.'

In Matthew's Gospel, today's passage follows Peter's declaration that Jesus is 'the Messiah, the son of the living God.' Peter liked the thought of Jesus as the Christ, the anointed one of God, sent to bring about the fulfilment of God's plan for the world. We like that, too.

What Peter could not handle was the fact that 'from that time on' Jesus started talking about suffering and death as his way of messiahship. Peter and we like our gods to be powerful, not suffering. More to the point, we like ourselves to be powerful, not suffering. God, however, sees things differently.

The pains, the crosses of our life, bring us to complain to God. In my own life, some of my most honest prayers have been at such times. No fancy words, no set phrases, just raw pain, confusion and anger. In other words, my true self.

Apparently, God prefers the complaints of Jeremiah to the solicitude of Peter. When Peter tries to head off talk of suffering, Jesus calls him 'Satan.'

Jesus says yet another shocking thing about Peter: 'You are a stumbling block to me.' How can Peter's hope that Jesus not suffer be a stumbling block?

Peter is renewing the temptation that Satan presented to Jesus at the start of his ministry, the temptation to avoid the painful way and take the easy way. Jesus is upset because it is a real temptation that Peter presents to him. The cross was Jesus' vocation, but that does not mean he liked it or did not hope for some other way. He prayed for as much in Gethsemane.

The temptation to avoid the cross is not one that Jesus alone faced. We, too, face it. That is the reason Jesus tells us that we must be willing to take up the cross. We, too, must face and overcome the temptation Jesus faced and overcame.

'If any want to become my followers, let them deny themselves and take up their cross and follow me.' He wants us to follow him to the cross and through the temptation to avoid it.

What is the cross? It is not merely the instrument of torture on which Jesus was killed. It is certainly more than a decoration or a piece of jewelry. The cross is the way in which God relates with the world.

We say that God is love, and that our lives are meant to be signs of that love for the world, but what is love?

Love is not merely the emotion that is a real part of every healthy human life. The kind of love that characterizes God is not an emotion, but an activity. It is a giving of one's all for the sake of the beloved. This is symbolized in Christian marriage, where the couple commit themselves to sharing not an emotion, but a life.

The ultimate self-emptying, the ultimate offering we can make in love, is the offering of our whole life. God did that in Jesus on the cross. If we want to know what God is like, we must look at the cross. If we want to show what God is like, we must take up our cross.

But, that has implications for us who call ourselves Christians. We must be willing to face the cross, willing to sacrifice even life itself for the sake of God and others. We do it knowing that in becoming like Christ on his cross we also become like him in his resurrection. As St. Paul says, 'If we have been united with him in a death like his, we will certainly be united with him in a resurrection like his.'

Does that mean we must go in search of opportunities to suffer? No. We need not search. They will come. What we must do is spend our lives facing the minor crosses that come our way, learning patience, humility and service. Then, when the big demands come, we will already have learned to deny ourselves and follow the Lord.

Then, we will be able to face the Lord in his glory and receive the reward of those who show the unlimited love of God to the world, unlimited life.

Twenty-Third Sunday of the Year (A)

The field of Biblical studies called Textual Criticism compares ancient manuscripts of the Bible to see where spelling mistakes, dropped words and added words may have changed texts. The differences are usually minor.

Today's Gospel passage from Matthew may include such a phrase. Some ancient manuscripts contain it, some do not. Was it dropped by some scribes (remember that until the 1450's all copies of Matthew were hand-written) or was it added? The scholars think it more likely in this case that the phrase was added.

That phrase is 'against you' in 'If another member of the church sins against you, go and point out the fault when the two of you are alone.' So, it is more likely that the original version is 'If another member of the church sins, go and point out the fault . . .'

The difference is not significant, since any sin against my brothers and sisters is a sin against me as well. However, when I expand my view to see sins against others as well as myself, I face questions of social justice. There is more to sin than ill-mannered interpersonal behavior. Anything that deprives people of their dignity as God's children or deprives them of realizing and exercising that dignity is sinful.

So, throughout history, believers have confronted those who sin against their brothers and sisters, sometimes with only a dim awareness of it. The prophets spoke strongly and often against the powerful. Someone today who heard or read the sermons and writings of the fathers of the Church without knowing they were more than a thousand years old might attack them as 'new-fangled mixing of the Church where it doesn't belong.' Medieval sermons, especially those preached to kings and nobles, frequently dealt with the abuses of power that enabled the powerful to oppress the weak.

In the abstract and in the past, it might be easy to accept the idea that the Church should be concerned with such issues. In fact, it seems to have been generally recognized that Christians should confront one another and their societies with the effects of sin in the community. However, nowadays when Christians or Churches try to follow the Lord's admonition to not let sin pass without our speaking up, the reaction can be very peculiar.

'The Church should be concerned with religion, not with society, economics or politics.' That phrase is often used by those who feel threatened by a call to repentance. For many Christians, 'morality' is merely concerned with sex; the justice or injustice of our society, our economy or our politics is not a religious issue.

Something new has happened to make relatively large numbers of Christians feel that concerns of faith are limited to prayer, good works and 'churchy' things. Ironically, considering the tradition of two thousand years, many of those people who have such a new attitude call themselves conservative.

This strange development is probably linked to something that is good, the improvement in the lives of millions of people. More people have more comfort, more security, more power and more of a vested interest in maintaining things pretty much as they are than has ever been the case before.

When calls for repentance, for social justice, for a really adequate provision for the poor were aimed at a king, the peasants could cheer, at least in their hearts. Now, many of the peasants' descendants are more comfortable than any king ever was. And we are as reluctant as kings to give up privileges and the means of acquiring them.

The Lord's command to confront sin in ourselves and others is never easy to fulfill. It is even harder, perhaps, to be the object of that confrontation, whether as individuals or as societies.

So, what are we to do?

For starters, we should learn to listen carefully to those who say we must change. They may be wrong; they may be right. We must listen to them to learn which.

On the other hand, we may be wrong. We must look honestly at ourselves and our society and see where we might betray many of God's children for the sake of a comparative few.

Then, we must take what steps we can (and they might not be big ones) to bring our world a bit closer to what we pray, that God's will be done on earth as in heaven.

The one thing we must not do is refuse to listen to the voices of those who accuse us and our world of sin.

Twenty-Fourth Sunday of the Year (A)

Genesis contains a fragment of a warrior's song attributed to Lamech, great-great-grandson of Cain. It is included to show the increase of violence due to the growth of the power of sin. 'I have killed a man for wounding me, a young man for striking me. If Cain is avenged sevenfold, truly Lamech seventy-sevenfold.' The desire for revenge is nothing new.

Jesus refutes Lamech's arithmetic. Rather than 490 measures of vengeance, the Lord calls for the same amount of forgiveness. It is not sufficient merely to refrain from vengeful words or deeds. Forgiveness, not seething resentment, is the opposite of vengeance.

Peter seems to have understood this, if only partly. That is why he asked Jesus how many times he should forgive. How much insult and injury must we endure before we are justified in taking revenge? But, Peter is not really asking, then, about forgiveness. He is asking how long we must postpone vengeance. If Peter were to truly forgive each time, he would always be starting his count at 'One.'

I have been hurt in various ways by others throughout my life. Family, friends, enemies and strangers have all done things that annoy, disappoint, damage or enrage me. I have forgotten most of those hurts and forgiven many. But, there remain not a few of the not-yet-forgiven or the seemingly unforgivable. Some offenses seem too great to let me forgive and forget them.

In the parable Jesus tells of an official who owes his master a huge sum of money. In fact, an impossible sum of money, ten thousand talents. Since there is also no way anyone could run up such a fantastic debt, it is clear that Jesus is using hyperbole, exaggeration, to make a point.

The point of this debtor's story is not the punishments the king would impose on him, since not even selling the official and his family as slaves would repay the debt. The point is the generosity of his forgiveness. An immeasurable offense is matched by immeasurably generous forgiveness.

The king is, of course, God who forgives our sins. The official? The official is everyone, including me. Does that mean that I have sinned against God to a fantastic degree? I hope not, though I know that some of the sins against me that I cannot or will not forgive in others were not great or even wrong in the mind of the sinner. It is also certain that I have hurt others without realizing it, or without intending the hurt I have caused.

Perhaps my sins against God are equivalent to ten thousand talents though I do not realize it. The point of the parable, though, is not the enormity of the offense, but the magnitude of the forgiving love. No matter how much of it I need, there is an infinite loving forgiveness available to me.

But, the parable does not end with the king's forgiveness. When the official sees someone who owes a few months' wages, he does not forgive. Though he has been forgiven an infinite amount, the official will not forgive a measurable sum.

That is my story. God's infinite love for me means infinite forgiveness of my sins. My too-finite love means limited forgiveness or no forgiveness at all for my fellows.

This is where my problem arises. The final message of the parable is that the infinitely forgiving love of God can be limited by only one thing: my unwillingness to imitate it. I even ask for that limitation each time I pray the Lord's Prayer, asking that we be forgiven as we have forgiven.

At first glance, this seems to result in a Catch-22 situation. I am commanded to forgive others because I have been forgiven, but I cannot be forgiven unless I forgive others first.

The way out of the paradox is to realize that forgiving and being forgiven is not a parade of activities that happen in order—God forgives, then I forgive, then God forgives. God's forgiving me and my forgiving others go on together. There is no progression, but a constant interactive experience. God's forgiveness and my own must become like a dance, with God's forgiving and mine moving together in a mirrored harmony.

Twenty-Fifth Sunday of the Year (A)

The parable of the workmen was probably included in Matthew's Gospel as a rebuke to Jewish Christians who resented the influx of Gentiles into the community. The Jews had generations of experience at believing in God. Jesus himself was one of them.

Then, from out of nowhere, all sorts of strange people started coming into the Church. Not only did they not come from a tradition of believing in God, many of them were in fact pagans who had recently elbowed their way into the community, claiming the right to be part of the chosen people of God. They spoke different languages, wore different clothes, ate different foods and had different customs.

Matthew's message is a reprimand to those who were uncomfortable with the newcomers.

In the parable, those hired early in the morning and those brought on near quitting time all receive the same welcome from the landowner and the same wage, a denarius. A denarius was the amount one needed to live for a day. So, the landowner gave each of the workers all they needed. Of course, the landowner represents God, who will give us all we need. In the Kingdom of God, we will not be given more than all we really need. Neither will we be given less.

So, the parable is not a story about labor relations or wage policies. It is about how God deals with the world. And yet, it is not totally unrelated to the concerns of the modern world.

All over the world, societies are facing their own version of what the early Church experienced. Migrant workers, refugees and immigrants are 'invading' areas where their races, cultures, religions, speech and customs are alien. They often face ridicule, exploitation, discrimination and even violence.

Another way in which 'outsiders' are becoming a strong presence in many societies is the refusal of women and minorities to remain outside the mainstream of their societies. People who have traditionally been in charge see their power eroded and are challenged to either cooperate or be ignored.

On a global level, nations and societies that in the past were merely objects of colonialism, tourism or exploitation for resources or cheap labor are demanding recognition and a just share of the gifts of the world.

In the Church, too, this phenomenon is arising, and not a few Christians appear threatened by the change, just as the Jewish Christians were long ago. If one wishes to survey Christianity today, the journey must begin in places like São Paulo, Nairobi and Manila rather than Rome or Canterbury.

The response to this on the part of many Christians is like that of the landowner in the parable. They work to ensure that all people have a fair share of the opportunities and goods of this world. They join the struggle for justice within societies, among nations and in the Churches.

Such activity is not always welcomed, even by fellow Christians. The imitators of the landowner are accused of abandoning the Church's spiritual mission for material aims, of being dupes of various enemies of society or religion and even traitors.

However, involvement in social criticism and activism by Christians is none of these. Christian calls for equal justice are not based upon ideology or a commitment to solely material values. We must be involved in order to show what God and God's Kingdom are like. The generosity of the landowner shows that God offers the same love to all. The generosity of Christians aims at doing the same. It is a spiritual mission, even when it looks similar to what others may do from a different motivation.

The Incarnation of Christ is God's declaration that if we wish to learn about God, we must look for signs of God's love in the world in which we live. This world is the place where the spiritual is meant to be visible. Just as the parables of Jesus show the love of God in stories about lost coins, vineyards and generous landowners, the followers of Jesus must make the events of everyday life point to God's loving presence among us.

Therefore, we must root out discrimination and an unwelcoming attitude in our own lives. In addition, as citizens, as members of society, we must use the structures and opportunities available to us to make the world more like the Kingdom of God, more like the field of the generous landowner.

Twenty-Sixth Sunday of the Year (A)

What sort of man do you imagine Jesus to be? Kind? Gentle? Good-humored? Intelligent? Powerful? Obnoxiously insulting?

Obnoxiously insulting? Jesus in today's Gospel passage is certainly so. Good manners and proper deference were in order when talking to the religious leaders of the people.

What does Jesus say that is so obnoxious? He certainly cannot and does not condemn the leaders because they violate the rules of their religion. They were scrupulous in fulfilling their duties. So, why compare them unfavorably with thieving, traitorous tax collectors and prostitutes?

The answer comes in the response of the sons in the parable to the task their father asks them to perform: 'Go work in the vineyard today.' One says that he will go; the other refuses. One son says the right thing, the other says the wrong.

The son who said the right thing is like the chief priests and elders of the people. They say all the right things. They teach. They fulfill all their public religious duties (for actions do, indeed 'say' something).

But, there is a problem. The son who says, 'I go, sir,' talks a good game, but is useless.

The other son, the one who refuses to go, changes his mind and eventually heads out to the vineyard. Jesus asks the priests and elders which son is actually the obedient one—the one who says the right thing or the one who does the right thing. The answer is plain. Deeds are more important than words.

Then, Jesus springs his insult. The son who says the right things, who looks right, stands for the good people listening to him. The son who looks and sounds disobedient at first glance represents the tax collectors and prostitutes. They, not the nice religious folks, are the ones who really do the will of God.

Does this mean that Jesus is in favor of sin? No. Remember that the right thing they did was to repent when John the Baptist came teaching the way of holiness. What, then, could this passage mean for us today?

In more ways than we might like to admit, we are like the son who said, 'Sure, Dad, anything you say.' In our Baptism, we have been given a call by God, a vocation to go out into the vineyard. In that same Baptism, we have said our 'Yes.'

Throughout our lives, we repeat that 'Yes' in various ways. We traipse off to church on Sunday. We take part in the prayers and hymns, recite the Creed and share the Sacrament. This yes-saying is probably sincere. But, is it enough? What about Tuesday or Thursday?

The test of Christian faith is not merely whether or not we are in church on Sunday. Going to church is the renewing of our 'yes' to the call of God. But, do we follow through on the promise?

What would it mean to actually go out into the vineyard and do the Father's will? Some of the things I should do are similar to what I do in church—prayer, reflection on the Word of God. Other things are, in fact, what I do in church, but they take more ambiguous forms outside. Sharing peace, for example. In the liturgy, it is a gesture. Outside in the vineyard, it may be a kind word, a helpful deed, a principled position.

The main focus of my yes-saying in church is the Eucharist, communion with God and the People of God. Taking that communion out to the vineyard means treating every person I meet as a brother or sister.

On the other hand, many people who do not say 'yes' with me on Sunday spend the week doing the will of God. The world would be a much worse place, a place even less a sign of the Kingdom of God than it is, were it not for the men and women who do not say yes to the Creed, to the Church or to the Sacraments but who live for others. They become workers in the vineyard, making it worthy of the Lord's ownership even though they do not know it and would object if told so.

Jesus presents tax collectors and prostitutes to the chief priests and elders of the people as a challenge to conversion. The same is true today. The men and women who without saying 'yes' to the Lord obey his will and bring the care and love of God to this love-starved world are a challenge to us.

Twenty-Seventh Sunday of the Year (A)

Today's gospel parable is clearly about Jesus, the Son who followed the prophets to the Master's vineyard Israel, and was killed. It is unusual in that it talks about Jesus himself, rather than focusing on the Kingdom of God.

The parable is obviously a critique of those to whom the Lord's vineyard, the People of God, has been entrusted, the religious leaders of Israel. They use and abuse the vineyard for their own purposes and not those of God. No matter how often God's prophets call them to repentance, they fail to respond. Even God's sending the Son does not move them.

So, responsibility for the People of God will be turned over to a new laborer, the Church.

The evangelist included this parable in order to give Gentile Christians confidence that their membership in the community of disciples was in accord with God's will. Gentiles were not always welcome because they were frequently unable or unwilling to follow all the Law of Moses. This parable tells them they are in the Church because God has handed that vocation to them.

Millennia have passed, and a parable that gave Gentile Christians a sense of vocation and legitimacy vis-a-vis the Jews does not have the same emotional force for us. So, what are we to make of the parable? Is it of merely historic interest?

Let's look at the comment of the chief priests and elders. Jesus asks them, 'When the owner of the vineyard comes, what will he do to those tenants?'

They answer: 'He will put those wicked ones to a miserable death, and lease the vineyard to other tenants who will give him the produce at the harvest time.' It is easy for them to recognize that the tenants are wicked. What they fail to recognize is that they themselves are the wicked tenants.

Could it be that we fail to see the same failure in ourselves?

The Church has its own chief priests and elders of the people. Are those called to the ministry of leadership in the Church always and everywhere good stewards of the trust they have been given? No.

That was easy to say. It is not untrue, but yet, might we not repeat the error of those who heard Jesus and recognized others' failings? There always have been, are and always will be bad leaders in the Church.

But who are the tenants of the vineyard of the Lord? Are they solely the clergy? We must think about where that vineyard is today. In Jesus' time, it was the People of God called Israel. Does that mean that today the vineyard is the People of God called the Church?

But, the whole world is called to the Kingdom of God. In that case, the laborers in the vineyard are not merely the leaders of the Church, but the Church itself.

That means that every Christian has the duty that once belonged to the chief priests and elders of the people. We are, each of us, members of the priestly people of God. Our vocation is to give guidance, correction and encouragement to all people that they may yield the harvest God longs for.

How can we do that? Preaching and teaching, explicitly declaring the loving will of God, is certainly one way, an essential one. But, the chief priests and elders of the people did that. It is more important that we practice what we preach. Our daily lives must be examples of living freely as sons or daughters of God.

The Eucharist is the supreme example of that. We (not a lonely I) share full communion with God in Jesus Christ. Carrying that communion into everyday life will draw others to that same communion. They will be a rich harvest.

There is one other thing we must do. We must hear and heed the messengers God sends to us workers in the vineyard. For we, too, need to be converted throughout our lives. We must be alert to the Lord's call to move beyond what we've always done to a deeper understanding, a more effective service. The first messenger is, of course, Christ in his Word and Church. But there will be others. We will recognize them if when they speak we see the sins of others. That will be a sign that we must look to our own.

Twenty-Eighth Sunday of the Year (A)

Ask someone who is not a Christian to describe the Church and its members. What words will you hear? Dedicated? Misled? Helpful? Fanatic? Generous? Strict? Honest? Rule-bound? Dependable? Superstitious? Mysterious? Judgmental? Hypocritical?—Many words, some more accurate than others.

Will you hear joyful? Good-humored? Fun to be with? Singing, dancing and playing?

Most Christians are probably marked by those things. But, they are not what come to the lips of outsiders when asked to describe us. In fact, would they come to the lips of most Christians?

If Jesus had not described the Kingdom of God as a wedding reception, then joy, good humor and fun need not be marks of the Christian. But, Jesus did describe the Kingdom that way.

If we are signs of the Kingdom, then perhaps we should look more like revelers than anything else. Sure, the world is a place of sin and suffering. But, it is also the gateway to the Kingdom that Jesus describes as a banquet to which everyone, bad as well as good, is invited.

So, must I become grimly determined to be happy, since it is my 'duty' as sign of the Kingdom? Actually, if I could recognize myself as grimly determined to be happy, the irony might help me develop a spark of humor that could make me a more cheerful believer in God who made monkeys, kittens, children and such a ridiculous creature as I.

Perhaps the reason I am not a reveling Christian is that I do not allow the Lord to show me not only what is in store for me, but what I have already.

Jesus has taught us to pray, 'Our Father.' If I paid more heed to those words, at the very least I would start giggling in embarrassment. 'Me—able to call God my daddy?!'

Then, there is the Eucharist. All it takes is a piece of bread and a sip of wine to put me in union with Christ's real presence in the world! Is solemnity the appropriate response to that, or is a child opening presents on Christmas morning the better model of Eucharistic spirituality?

In the Eucharist, in the worship and service of the community of good and bad folks that Jesus invites to the banquet of God's Kingdom, I am offered a foretaste of heaven. How could I do other than rejoice?

And what of the joyous gifts God has given me— friends, family, children on the street, good art, good music, good books, good food? When I really look at all this, really give thanks for them, I rejoice in God's unbelievable generosity. What did I do to deserve all this?

Nothing. It's all a free gift. All this, and heaven too! Even my pains and confusion, my doubt and my death are embraced by God.

Is it any wonder that 'the source and summit of the Christian life' is called Eucharist, Thanksgiving?

So, how can I increase my wonder, my grateful joy in God's love? The first step is probably to open my eyes to the wonders around me and realize that they are all gifts for me from a Father who is madly in love with me.

The next step is probably to take it easy. The world and the Church will probably survive if for the next week I refrain from being either a dutiful Christian or feeling guilty because I am a shirker. As time allows (and there is usually time to do what we really want to do), let's take pleasant walks, listen to good music, read a good book, enjoy good food and drink, waste time with a friend.

And the best friend to waste time with is Jesus himself. Each day, set aside some quiet time (10 minutes or more) to just sit comfortably still. Don't worry if your thoughts wander. The Asian spiritual masters call that our monkey mind and disparage it, but what's wrong with monkeys, 'the craziest people'?

At the end of the time, tell a joke or funny story to Jesus. It need not be 'appropriate,' just funny. Tell it out loud. That may make you feel foolish, and that can be the beginning of merriment with the Lord.

We may as well get used to being merry with him, since he's inviting us to spend eternity at a joyous banquet with him.

Twenty-Ninth Sunday of the Year (A)

The Pharisees and Herodians put a touchy political question to Jesus. The Pharisees desired an end to Roman rule in their homeland. The Herodians, on the other hand, were whole-hearted supporters of cooperation with Rome. Cooperation brought benefits; opposition would bring destruction.

By going to Jesus together, they are trying to catch him in a political web. If he were to answer with the Herodian position that the Romans were a legitimate authority, Jesus could be branded a traitor to his people. On the other hand, if he were to say that the Romans had no authority to collect taxes, he would be liable to arrest by them.

Jesus sidesteps the question by merely saying that since the money belongs to Caesar in the first place, they should give it back to him. Jesus does not answer the question of political legitimacy. He seems unconcerned with who's on top.

Yet, his question to the questioners contains an important message. 'Whose image is this and whose inscription?' Coins were decorated with the image of the ruler and an inscription giving his name and title.

The Pharisees and Herodians answer that the image is that of the Roman emperor, Tiberius. So, Jesus tells them to 'give therefore to the emperor the things that are the emperor's and to God the things that are God's.'

The image of Tiberius determines what belongs to Tiberius. What then determines what belongs to God? Again, an image. Whatever bears the image of God belongs to God and should be given to God.

Humans have been described in various ways. But for God humankind is the image of God.

The image of God— that's you and me. But, not only that, it's also *them*.

You know who they are. The different people. Different races. Different religions. Different nations. Different gender. Different sexual orientation. Different political views. Different physical abilities. Different economic systems. Different moral (or immoral) behavior.

The past century has been one of unparalleled horror. And most of that horror has been caused by what may be the greatest of all sins against God the Creator. The sin has many names —racism, chauvinism, sexism, agism, exploitation—but it is basically one sin, the denial of God's claim to have 'created humankind in his own image.'

Having denied that certain people are the image of God, we have sacrificed them to a variety of Caesars—individuals like Stalin, Hitler or Mao; ideologies like communism, manifest destiny or racial purity; nations in chauvinistic 'patriotism'; gender images as in abuse of women or 'gay bashing'; economic power as in exploitive capitalism and so many more.

Even my own little versions of such sin are horrible, because they deny the will of God in creation. Too often, my refusal to see others as the image of God prevents their own realization of their dignity.

We too often refuse to see that our differences—no matter how great they appear— are minor variations of an image, the image of God.

Is the image of God about looks? Of course not. Our variety tells us it cannot be about looks. It is about a vocation, a vocation to resemble God in loving others.

Perhaps the reason I forget that all women and men are the image of God is that I forget that I am made in that image, too. I am too self-centered to give much thought to being a creature, someone made by Another according to a particular model.

That model is Christ, the absolutely perfect image of God.

The more I become like Christ, the more I can see the image of God in myself and all other people and rejoice that our many differences still do not completely exhaust the possibilities of that image. We may mar it, but we cannot erase it. We may make it as glorious as an angel, yet we cannot express it fully.

We Christians have been shown Christ, the image of God, so that we can proclaim that image to all the world. In order to do so, we must clear away whatever mars that image in us. That includes all those sins that deny the creation of humanity—all men and women—in the image of God. It includes giving Caesar in all his manifestations no more than his little due.

Thirtieth Sunday of the Year (A)

The Sadducees were fundamentalists. They only believed what their Bible told them. Since that Bible did not mention resurrection, the Sadducees denied it. The Pharisees, on the other hand, were open to the development of hitherto unthought-of implications of their faith. So, they believed in resurrection.

When Jesus showed that he opposed the Sadducee position regarding resurrection, the Pharisees may have thought they had an ally. So, they gave him the dignity of asking him a typical rabbinical question about the Law.

There were 613 laws, and obviously some were more important than others. Some were keys to interpreting the others. But, which were the most important? Opinions varied. One could learn a lot about a rabbi by knowing which ones he considered 'heavy' or serious, and which 'light.'

The lawyer asked Jesus his opinion on what constituted the heaviest of the laws. Jesus answered as most Jews then and now would, with words from the *Shema*, the Jewish profession of faith. 'Hear, O Israel: the Lord is our God, the Lord alone. You shall love the Lord your God with all your heart, and with all your soul and with all your might.'

The second law that Jesus cites is another that would not have struck his hearers as unusual. Others had linked the two. 'You shall love your neighbor as yourself.'

However, there are two things that Jesus says that are new, things that tell us the basis of his faith, teaching and activity.

The first is that the two commandments are equivalent. Love of God is shown in love of neighbor and love of neighbor shows itself in love of God. When it comes to the most basic love, you can't have love of God without love of neighbor and you can't have love of neighbor without love of God.

How can this be? God is God, and people are people. How can loving one be loving the other? The answer is in the Incarnation of Christ. When the Father sent the Son to be one of us, this world, every part of it and everyone in it, became the place where God is to be known and loved. God is not loved in the abstract, but in the concrete details of our daily lives.

But, if we grant that the way to love God is to love our neighbor, that still leaves a question. How is it possible to say that we can only love our neighbor by loving God? After all, there are atheists who love their neighbor without ever mentioning God.

Unbelievers may not know or accept a relationship with God, but they have one nonetheless, and their faithfulness to that relationship constitutes love of God and is, unbeknownst to themselves, the basis for their love of neighbor.

The second striking thing that Jesus says is that 'On these two commandments the whole law is based, and the prophets as well.' The only way to understand Scripture, the only way to understand any revelation of God, is by means of these two commandments.

This brings us back to the Sadducees. Their way to understand revelation was to look at words. They failed to look with love at God who is behind those words. Had they done so, they would have known that God's life-giving love cannot be overcome by death. Love is the way to heaven.

I cannot be absolutely sure that I am loving God. That is why Jesus' making love of God and love of neighbor equivalent is so wonderful. If I am loving my neighbor, I am loving God. And, if I fail to love my neighbor, whatever I may say, think or feel to the contrary, I am not loving God.

Love of neighbor (and therefore, love of God) is not mainly a matter of feelings. Feelings are part of it all, especially gratitude—that is the reason our celebration of love is called Eucharist, Thanksgiving. But love is first and foremost a decision to put oneself at the practical service of another.

The First Epistle of John asks us, 'How does God's love abide in anyone who has the world's goods and sees a brother or sister in need and yet refuses to help?'

The law of Christ is simple. Love. Love God by loving your neighbor. And your neighbor is anyone close enough to be loved, anyone in the world.

Thirty-First Sunday of the Year (A)

The Church seems self-contradictory at times. For two millennia, we have proclaimed the words of Jesus that say that there should be no titles among his followers. Usually, the proclaimers are addressed as 'Reverend,' 'Pastor,' 'Father,' 'My Lord,' 'Your Excellency,' 'Your Eminence,' or 'Your Holiness.'

The problem for Jesus is a style of piety that attempts to substitute appearances for real faith and faithfulness. Jesus criticizes the scribes and Pharisees not because of what they teach, but because they are unwilling to practice what they preach. They like being teachers and being called 'rabbi,' but their religion is more show than substance.

We all know people who make it easy to know their religion. A Christian may wear a cross. A Jew might dress a certain way. A Muslim may have a calloused forehead from rubbing it against a prayer rug. These people are not necessarily hypocrites. They may be giving witness to their faith. They may not even be concerned with whether or not others notice, bearing the external marks of their religion as a way of reminding themselves of who they are and how they should behave.

'How they should behave' is the key. Behavior is what gives validity to the external signs of religious faith. When Jesus tells us to let our light shine, it is not supposed to be a spotlight on ourselves, but one that allows others to see our good works.

It is more important that God be praised than that I be praised. It is more important that men and women hear and see the Kingdom of Heaven proclaimed than it is that they notice who does the proclaiming.

Most of us know this and struggle against the sin of pride in our Christian life. However, even though we may recognize the danger in ourselves of ostentatious religiosity that draws attention to ourselves rather than God, we frequently fail to realize that we sometimes encourage and abet it in others.

The scribes and the Pharisees loved 'to have the place of honor at banquets and the best seats in the synagogues, and to be greeted with respect in the marketplaces, and to have people call them rabbi.' But, someone gave them those seats, someone greeted them, someone called them rabbi.

The practice continues. Clergy (and religious) receive special treatment more often than not, the sort of treatment one might give an imbecile demigod, one who is semi-divine, but incapable of handling the normal demands of life—like picking up a restaurant check.

And, like the scribes and Pharisees of old, many of the objects of special treatment rather like life on a pedestal. Some even expect such treatment. They themselves become the 'heavy burdens, hard to bear.'

There are others who try to climb down from the pedestal upon which people put them. But people try to shove them back. Why is that? Why do so many people want their clergy to be specially treated and insulated from life? Is it a bribe?

If so, what do people gain by their deference, their greetings, their special treatment toward religious leaders? In the case of the scribes and Pharisees, they sat 'on Moses' seat.' That is, they spoke with authority about the Law of God. Might people think similarly of Christian clergy?

In bribing the preachers, do we unconsciously hope to bribe God? Are we looking for some sort of payback from God? Or, perhaps we are hoping that by putting preachers outside the responsibilities of everyday life, we can keep them from applying the Word of God to those situations of our everyday lives where we'd rather not have to hear what God expects of us.

What shall we do? Most of us can do little about clergy who imitate the scribes and Pharisees. Settling for the material and emotional 'perks' of ministry and missing the spiritual excitement and rewards of real service is their self-inflicted punishment.

We can, however, see what we do to perpetuate the semi-deification of the clergy. For starters, imagine asking a bishop, priest or minister to help wash the dishes. If the thought startles you, ask why it does and if it should.

An aside: Many people wonder why some Churches address their clergy as 'Father' even though it is apparently forbidden in the Gospel.

The rationale is that the clergy are not being put on a par with God the Father, and so there is no violation of the Lord's mandate. The title is used by analogy with physical fatherhood, and even the most stringent fundamentalists call their male parent 'father.'

Baptism is a new birth, and in recognition of the fact that we are born anew, the one who is the usual instrument of this birth is addressed as a parent. So, the title declares something about all Christians rather than merely the one addressed.

Thirty-Second Sunday of the Year (A)

The moral attached to today's parable does not suit the story. 'Keep awake therefore, for you know neither the day nor the hour.' The foolish virgins slept, but after all, so did the wise ones. Sleep was not what separated the wise from the fools.

In fact, it would be difficult to see much difference between the two groups until the bridegroom's arrival. They were probably dressed much alike. All of them carried lamps. All of them nodded off.

Just as the wise virgins did not seem at first sight to differ from the foolish, we Christians, generally speaking, do not at first sight seem to differ from our neighbors. We may not even be wiser than they.

The wise virgins were not vigilant, straining their eyes in the dark to see the approach of the bridegroom. Like the foolish virgins, they fell asleep. The difference was that the wise virgins were ready for what would come. They had their oil.

If we look like our neighbors, and do so much that is like what they do, is the difference that we have our oil ready? That the bridegroom might surprise us, but we are ready for action when he does?

Who is the bridegroom? At first glance, we might think that he is Christ, and that we must be ready to welcome his coming in our lives. But, while we must be ready to meet the Lord, this parable is not about Jesus himself, but about the kingdom of God. 'The kingdom of heaven will be like this,' is the way Jesus introduces the parable. He is speaking of the answer to our prayer, 'your kingdom come.'

What is the kingdom? We do not know the details, since it is beyond all that we can imagine or experience in our present life. But we have hints. From the Lord's Prayer, we know that it involves God's will being done, that all we need to sustain life will be given and that forgiveness will be shared. We know it is the reality of life beyond death. From the Eucharist, our deepest experience of the kingdom in this life, we know it means total communion with Christ in offering praise to the Father.

Ultimately, the kingdom is not something to know, but something to experience. So, we pray for that experience, for God to finish the work of salvation.

But, it's taking a long time. Even when we peer vigilantly into the darkness of our world, we don't always see signs that God is coming to us. At times, it seems as if God is not coming at all, that there might not even be a God to come. So we nap, nap without being ready for the kingdom's coming.

Because we do that, when the kingdom does come in its little precursors, we are not ready to recognize it, any more than a virgin with a burnt-out lamp can recognize the groom in the gloom.

Those little precursors are the acts of love and forgiveness that we see around us. They are the people who are not overcome by the darkness, but who carry on with faith and hope, confident that in God's good time they will know that they have been eternally embraced by God.

In order to see and greet these hints of the kingdom, we need to have oil prepared for our lamps. But what is the oil? Lamp oil helps us see in the dark. We need an oil that will enable us to see the coming of the kingdom in our dark world of sin, confusion, suffering and death.

The first way to acquire that oil is through prayer. By spending time becoming friends with God, we learn to recognize the divine footfalls in the darkness of our lives.

The Word of God in Scripture, especially as it is proclaimed in the community of those who wait and pray for the coming of the kingdom, is another source of oil.

Finally, we should keep in mind the words of the British writer George Orwell, 'To see what is in front of one's nose needs a constant struggle.' Signs of God's kingdom are all around us. If we remember that, we will see them and thus build up our supply of oil so that at any time, in any way that God comes to us, we will be ready.

Thirty-Third Sunday of the Year (A)

Since the talent was a sum beyond anyone's most avaricious dreams, Jesus seems to have liked using it in parables as a metaphor for the infinite love of God.

In today's parable, the master entrusts to his servants a total of eight talents, such an incredible amount that there could be no mistaking the master for anyone but God.

Fourteenth-century translations of Matthew introduced the word 'talent' into English, and within a century, the word took on the meaning we usually give it today, an aptitude or ability.

So, a word that once awed people with the immeasurable generosity of God shifted focus. Now, when we hear the word talent, we think not of God, but of ourselves.

The shift was based upon the interpretation of the parable. The master gives each of his servants a sum of money to use. In the same way, God gives each of us life, abilities and opportunities. Some of us use them to increase the measure of God's glory, others do not.

Talents are a treasure, but a responsibility as well. The master is angry with the servant who buries what he received. True, he did not lose it, but he was entrusted with a talent in order to put it to work for the master, not to bury it.

In the Middle Ages, people recognized that the parable was not a once-upon-a-time story, but was about themselves. God has given each of us an inestimable treasure. Calling it by the parable's name for treasure made sense.

However, care is needed using the word. We tend to think of talents as personal possessions and reasons to be praised. We forget that they are not ours, but God's. Whatever talents I have are given to me in trust to be used on God's behalf. I did not make, or even choose, my talents. I merely have use of them.

Does that mean that my talents are insignificant? Of course not. They are gifts from God, a treasure beyond counting. I can use them, abuse them, or bury them as I choose. God will want an accounting, but will not force me to use them in any particular way.

We often speak of trusting God, but today, we are reminded that God trusts us as well. Treasures the world desperately needs have been given to me. No one else has the exact same combination of talents. My talents can be used to fulfill the will of God or even thwart it. Not a single talent is worth less than an uncountable treasure.

We usually consider certain things as talents and overlook others. Artistic or academic ability will get me recognized as talented. But, there are so many other talents that we fail to recognize or take for granted, failing to assign them near-infinite value.

No one is without talents. No matter how weak and fractured the image of God may seem in us, no matter how severe our disabilities, by the very fact that we have life, we know we have talents. Affection is a talent. Service is a talent. Generosity is a talent. The ability to evoke and facilitate the talents of others is a talent. Not talents in the Hollywood sense, but talents in the heaven sense.

In fact, our 'drawbacks' may be our most precious talents, just as Jesus' cross was his glorification. For some people, perhaps suffering is a share in Christ's talent.

We should cultivate an ability to recognize talents, our own and others'. When we do that, two things happen. The first is that in recognizing talents, we can better put them to use for God's kingdom. Overlooked talents may become buried talents. The second is that we begin to understand the generosity of God.

That leads us back to seeing that talent is more about God's generosity than about us. My talents are nothing to brag about any more than breathing is something to brag about. When I use them in a praiseworthy way, the praise may be given to me, but it really belongs to God.

And how do I use the talents God has given me in a praiseworthy way? They are entrusted to me for the sake of the world, as a sign of God's generosity, so I must use them for the sake of the world. It is to us as servants and for the sake of being servants that God gives us talents. Let us not bury them, but put them forth for the whole world.

Thirty-Fourth or Last Sunday of the Year, Christ the King (A)

'If you look at a thing nine hundred and ninety-nine times, you are perfectly safe; if you look at it the thousandth time, you are in frightful danger of seeing it for the first time.'

That comment by GK Chesterton suits my experience with today's famous and popular passage about the final judgment.

I have looked at the text of today's Gospel many times. For a long time, I was 'perfectly safe' in doing so. I had it all figured out, and it was a comforting, though challenging message.

We will be judged by Christ on the basis of what we do to serve the poor, the weak, the lost and the lonely. Salvation would be bought by my doing things for others, obeying the law of service. Enough carrots peeled at the soup kitchen, enough visits to the sick, enough hoarseness at a demonstration, and I would be one of Christ's sheep.

But, I began to have some doubts. Perhaps I was nearing the eight hundredth look. The difficulty was the response of the righteous: 'Lord, when was it that we saw you hungry and gave you food, or thirsty and gave you something to drink? And when was it that we saw you a stranger and welcomed you, or naked and gave you clothing? And when was it that we saw you sick or in prison and visited you?'

I could understand why the goats might not recognize Jesus because of their spiritual blindness, but how could his own people not recognize him? How could those who followed him, heard his word, lived his law of love and shared his Eucharist not know him?

Obviously, I had to take another look. Finally, it occurred to me that the reason the righteous sheep did not recognize Christ was the fact that they had not known him in the first place. Matthew was not telling us about the judgment of Christians, but of non-Christians, those who serve Christ without knowing him by serving their neighbors. It was comforting to know that Christ would welcome those who did not believe in him.

What that meant for us Christians was that we had to be even more active, more busy earning our salvation because we have no excuse for not recognizing Christ in the 'least.' So, the judgment of Christians would be a sterner affair. We had to do even more serving or we would find ourselves lined up somewhere behind the goats.

For a hundred looks or so, that was enough.

But, I was getting beyond the nine hundredth look. Things began to look unfair toward us Christians. Unbelievers could get by with good deeds like a bunch of Boy Scouts. We seemed to need extraordinary deeds. What was the advantage of following Christ when salvation was easier for outsiders?

So, more thinking. I eventually realized that my salvation does not depend upon what I do, upon the prerequisites I meet, but upon the love of God. It is in meeting Christ and being embraced by him that we are saved. We do not do good in order to be saved, but because God's love is so overwhelming that we cannot help sharing it.

By now, my looks were getting into the nine hundred eighties or nineties, dangerous territory.

I began to wonder about those 'littlest ones.' Who are they? At first it seemed obvious. They are anyone who suffers hunger, thirst and all the other pains of humanity. Then, the nine hundred ninety-ninth look.

I realized that in Matthew's Gospel, 'little ones' has a very specific meaning. The little ones are not the weak and suffering. They are Christians, the followers of Jesus.

Does that mean that unbelievers are judged by what they do for us Christians? At first thought, that might be nice. That thought did not last long, however. If they serve us, it will be because we are so woebegone that they are moved to pity by us. One thousand!

We must be such followers of the crucified Jesus, giving our strength and even our lives for the sake of others that they will respond to us as the bystander at the crucifixion did who tried to give Jesus something to drink. When we become the little ones, they will serve Christ.

What does that mean for me and for the Church?

Maybe I should have stopped at the nine hundred ninety-ninth look.

First Sunday of Lent (A)

The Lenten readings for the first year of the three-year cycle of readings we use in the liturgy emphasize the fact that Lent is a season of preparation for catechumens who will be baptized at Easter and a season of renewal for the already-baptized who will reaffirm their own baptismal commitment. Some of the readings are unique in that they should be used in any year that there are catechumens in the community.

In the course of five weeks, we reflect upon the temptation of Christ, his transfiguration, his meeting with a woman at a well, his healing of a man born blind and his raising of Lazarus. Each teaches a different aspect of Baptism.

So, what has today's Gospel passage got to do with Baptism? More specifically, what has it to do with *my* Baptism, whether past or pending?

Is the Christian life easy or difficult? Considering that it entails a life-long struggle against temptation, it is difficult. Considering that it entails a life-giving awareness of the forgiving love of God, it is easy. If God has created me to live a certain way, why do I find it difficult to live the kind of life God calls me to?

Something is very wrong. I continually make choices that seem based upon the mistaken belief that what is bad for me is better, or at least easier, than my true good.

The temptation that Jesus faced is, in fact, the temptation I face. It was a temptation to take the easy way out. Jesus was hungry and tired after his fast. To go for the 'quick fix,' to take no responsibility for his actions and leave everything up to God, to grab for power—we all face similar temptations. We disguise laziness as faith. We disguise irresponsibility as hope. We disguise lust for power as love.

Basically, there is only one temptation, the temptation to betray my vocation. The vocation of Jesus was to face rejection and the cross. The devil offered him a way out, tempting Jesus with ways to avoid the suffering that his vocation entailed: 'You face hunger, danger and ineffective powerlessness? Come to me!'

What is my vocation? Paradoxically, temptation may help me find it. If the basic temptation I face is to betray the very purpose God has given to my existence, then looking at my temptations may give me hints of God's will for me.

One of the values of the Sacrament of Penance is that it gives me opportunities to reflect upon temptations in my life and take an honest look at those to which I give in. If I do more than merely compile a list of sins, but look for the underlying reasons for my sin, I may come to see patterns in my life, patterns that show the paths by which I try to get away from or get around the vocation God has given me. If I trace those paths back, I may find out the kind of person the devil would rather not have me be.

A broad hint of that vocation can be found in the Renunciations we make at our Baptism and when renewing our Baptismal commitment: 'Do you reject sin so as to live in the freedom of God's children?'

Baptism is a rejection of sin in our lives. It is uniting ourselves with Christ who sent the devil on its way when he refused to give in to temptation. What we reject is anything that prevents our living in the freedom of God's children.

That is my basic vocation, to be a child of God, free to grow, to love, to serve. Free to reject the glamour of evil, refusing to be mastered by sin. I will have a unique way to live that vocation, just as you will.

This, then, is the aspect of Baptism that the Gospel tells us of today. When we accept Christ's call to union with him in the Church, we commit ourselves to spurning the enticements of evil that would lessen our freedom as sons and daughters of God.

Lent is, then, among other things, an opportunity to prepare to make that renunciation at Easter by examining myself to find out where in my life temptation finds it easy to take root. Then, through prayer, fasting, reflection and works of mercy that break down my self-centeredness, I make in deeds the renunciation I will make in words as we celebrate the Resurrection.

Second Sunday of Lent (A)

In his classic work of theology, *The Idea of the Holy*, Rudolf Otto says that the basis of religion is an experience of spiritual power that overwhelms our day-to-day understanding and life. Otto speaks of our reaction to such encounters with holiness with the Latin phrase *mysterium tremendum et fascinans*. That is, we find divinity to be something beyond our understanding that is awe-inspiring yet attractive.

Today's Gospel passage illustrates Otto's point. Peter, James and John go with Jesus 'up on a high mountain by themselves.' This brings to mind Moses, who went up on Mount Sinai to meet with God. While atop the mountain, the disciples see Jesus, the carpenter-turned-preacher whom they have been following, revealed to them in glory. 'He was transfigured before them, and his face shone like the sun, and his clothes became dazzling white.'

Moses and Elijah, epitomes of the Law and the Prophets and therefore of the whole of Scripture, join Jesus. He is the fulfilment of the will and promise of God.

Peter's first reaction is fascinated attraction. 'Lord, it is good for us to be here.' But, when the full import of what he is experiencing dawns upon him, things change.

A bright cloud overshadows them. The voice of God comes from the cloud and 'when the disciples heard this, they fell to the ground and were overcome with fear.' Fear is a common reaction in the Bible to encounters with God's presence. Isaiah, Zechariah, Mary, the shepherds at Bethlehem and the women at the tomb of Jesus are just a few more of the many people who experience fear.

Fear is different from fright or terror. Fear as we understand it from Scripture is a sense of awe, of our weakness and insignificance.

CS Lewis likens it to the feeling someone might have when standing at the base of a tall cliff. It is basically an honest appraisal of ourselves when faced with the overwhelming power and goodness of God. Our prayer, 'Lord, I am not worthy,' before receiving the Eucharist is an example of it.

We have gone to the moon. We have turned the atom into a power source as we once did with fire and the horse. We have killed millions. We are driving species to extinction. There seems to be little or nothing before which we need kneel in awe. We are hard to impress. If we had been with Jesus at the mountain of the Transfiguration, we would have been too busy tweeting to either feel attraction or fear.

What has this to do with Lent and our preparation for baptisms and the renewal of baptismal commitments at Easter?

Like Peter, James and John, we have been invited by Christ to know him as he truly is, the Lord, the Son of God. Others may consider him a notable teacher, someone to be admired and, perhaps, emulated. We, however, have been called to see his glory, his holiness.

In our Baptismal profession of faith, we are asked if we 'believe in God, the Father almighty,' the *mysterium tremendum*. We answer, 'I do.' Then, we are asked to declare our belief in 'Jesus Christ, his only son,' the *mysterium fascinans*. Again, we answer, 'I do.'

My faith in Christ is more than a commitment to certain teachings or membership in a group that carries on various 'religious activities.' It is a relationship with God, a grateful response to the fact that the all-powerful ruler of the universe has invited me to kneel in awe at a love that embraces me and leads me in a fascinating man, Jesus Christ.

The Transfiguration reminds me of the mystery that Jesus, the fully human one, is also God. If I would know what it is to be truly human, I must look to Jesus. If I would know God, I must look to Jesus.

And to the Church. Not the Church as an institution, but to the Church as the People of God, the community of those who have been invited by Jesus to join him on the mountain, who have been united with Christ in Baptism and made sharers in his glory.

In every Christian the *mysterium tremendum et fascinans* is present. We hide it by our sin. We fail to see it because we fail to seek it. But, it is there because Christ is there. It is even present in myself. In our Baptism, we become signs of God to the world. We are the Transfiguration today.

Third Sunday of Lent (A)

Christians engage in many activities. We build places of worship. We conduct rituals. We pray. We theologize and teach. We have commandments and customs. We go on pilgrimages. We use various objects and images. We have publicly recognized leaders in the community. We have monasticism and mysticism. We have fund raising and do works of charity. We pray. We fast. We dance. We sing.

In other words, we do the same things as followers of other religions. Obviously, what makes Christianity unique is not to be found in such activities.

The basic difference between Christianity and other religions is an acknowledged relationship with God in and through Jesus Christ. Certainly, all people and all creation have a relationship with God in and through Jesus Christ, but Christians have accepted God's invitation to live in the knowledge of that relationship.

Some theologians would say that Christianity is not even a religion. They feel it is more accurate to say that Christianity has religious elements attached to it, but because of the relationship upon which it is based, it is basically so different as to be in a separate class from religions. That position makes sense, but whether we consider Christianity to be a religion or to merely have religious-looking aspects, let us look at what makes it look like a religion to outsiders.

So, what activity is unique to Christianity when viewed as one among many religions?

To be baptized, to be a Christian, means that one not only does 'religious' things—worship, meditation, study, service etc—but that one is first and foremost united with Christ and is therefore an evangelizer, a missioner as he was and is.

Today's Gospel passage is the one of this year's Lenten readings that brings the relationship between Baptism and mission to the fore.

The first evangelizer at the well as in our lives is Jesus. When he meets the woman, he does not hesitate to speak with her. Rabbis avoided contact with women. Jews avoided dealing with Samaritans and to accept food or drink from one was to risk impurity. John later presents even more reason for Jesus to avoid this particular woman— she is a notorious sinner.

The woman is shocked: 'How is it that you, a Jew, ask a drink of me, a woman of Samaria?' So are his disciples: 'They were astonished that he was talking with a woman.' But, this is the heart of evangelization. Jesus showed that God's love has no limits by breaking the limits of custom, propriety and even religious purity.

This is the source of the missionary vocation that each Christian shares with Christ by reason of Baptism. Mission comes from being known by Christ and accepted by him regardless of who we are.

The way in which he does this in the case of the woman is important. He invites her to break the same limits of custom that he has broken. When he asks her for water, he is giving her her first chance to evangelize, to share God's caring love. He is willing to share his vocation with her. (This is the reason evangelization includes the call to Baptism, to membership in the Church—we wish to share the missionary essence our vocation with all.)

The woman does not stop with giving Jesus some water to drink. As she comes to realize the extent to which Jesus has loved her, she leaves him to evangelize others. 'Then the woman left her water jar and went back to the city. She said to the people, "Come and see a man who told me everything I have ever done!" He knew her, yet loved her.'

Christ has not called me to be a disciple because of any goodness I have to offer or because I have talents that might be useful to the Kingdom. As St Paul tells us in the Epistle to the Romans, 'God proves his love for us in that while we were still sinners Christ died for us.'

To accept that love and to be baptized is to accept as well the vocation that Christ has from the Father, a vocation he chooses to share with me. That is, the vocation to be an evangelizer, a missioner.

I do not have to wander the world looking for opportunities to fulfill that vocation. I can find them even over a glass of water.

Fourth Sunday of Lent (A)

Insight means being clear-sighted enough to see the obvious. The man healed by Jesus in today's gospel has it: 'I know this much: I was blind before; now I can see.'

Being united with Christ through Baptism is to receive the gift of insight. We know we have insight because we know what the world is really all about. It is the place where God does wonders of love. Not the least of those wonders is healing the blindness that keeps us from seeing the truth.

The man who was blind since birth is a model of a Christian. When the he stands before his judges, he is an example of the Christian standing before the world, proclaiming Jesus, light of the world, at the risk of ostracism.

Until we meet Christ, we are like that man was in that we have not known light. We may think we see, as the Pharisees did, but we do not really see.

The man's vision of Jesus develops. This parallels the process by which someone moves from being an inquirer to a catechumen and eventually comes to Baptism. Even those who have been baptized in infancy probably go through much the same development in the course of their catechesis and life.

At first, he speaks of 'that man they call Jesus.' At his next interrogation, he declares that Jesus is a man 'from God.' Finally, when he has been driven out because of his growing insight, he calls Jesus 'Lord.'

Coming to see who Jesus is constitutes true enlightenment. Knowing who he is, we finally know the true story of the creation into which he came. We can see what is in front of us, and recognize it.

What do we see? What is it that should be so obvious to the followers of Christ yet is missed by others? God. All people have the possibility of seeing something of God. However, without seeing Jesus Christ, one cannot know God in the fullest revelation. To see Jesus is to see God and to know something of God that can be known in no other way.

The call to Baptism is an invitation to be cured of the blindness that afflicts the world. But, why us? Why should I be chosen to know the Lord when billions of better people than I will never have that chance?

Perhaps I need it more than others. Perhaps without the eye-opening experience of knowing Christ my blindness would be worse than that of the Pharisees. In the First Book of Samuel, it is not the strong and good-looking older sons of Jesse who are chosen. It is the runt of the pack, the youngest boy who is not even important enough to be under consideration. He is as unlikely to be a king as a blind man is to be a teacher of true sight to the religious experts.

Yet, it is David who is chosen. It is the man blind since birth who becomes the teacher. It is I who am called to see God in Christ. Unlikely, but God's ways are not ours.

How can I respond to this choice? The man in the Gospel can enlighten me here. He does the two things that define a Christian.

First, he proclaims Christ, standing up for him before the world, arguing his case and suffering on his behalf. In other words, the man says what he sees. This may help others realize their blindness and lead them to the eye-opening experience of knowing Christ. On the other hand, it may confirm some in their complacency.

Second, 'he said, 'I do believe, Lord,' and bowed down to worship him.' The healed man not only told others what he believed, he said it to Christ as well and adored.

Grateful courage is what underlies his actions. He knows that he needed to be cured and has been cured, and he knows who did it. He is not afraid to state that obvious truth.

Proclamation and worship are the essence of the Christian life.

When I reflect upon my call as one who has undeservedly been healed of the blindness that prevents our knowing God, I, too, should be moved to that same sort of grateful courage. I, too, should be a worshiping proclaimer.

Fifth Sunday of Lent (A)

The story of Lazarus is our story. The Lord says to all of us, 'Come to me!'

Today the catechumens take the last liturgical steps before their Baptism at the Easter Vigil. They have prepared themselves for a new life with Christ in the Church, and the Church is preparing itself to welcome them and renew our own baptismal commitment.

The raising of Lazarus is a reminder that to be a Christian is not just to live in a certain way. Christians do have customs and commands that we obey and disobey, the chief among them being to love God and all those whom God loves. But, the Christian life is not based upon those laws or defined by them; those laws are based upon something else that we are called to reflect upon today.

We love God because God loves us. Our love is a response. That is the reason that the mission of the Church is to show others the love of God. Only when they have experienced God's love can they come to love God themselves.

God's love is not limited in any way. I can sin, and God forgives me, saying, 'Come to me!' I can wander off, and God goes with me, saying 'Come to me!' I can suffer, and God suffers with me, saying, 'Come to me!' I can die, and God, who died with me in Christ, says, 'Come to me!'

We started Lent with the Ash Wednesday reminder, 'Remember, you are dust, and to dust you will return.' Death is the most powerful force we know. It comes to all, and puts an end to all. It makes a mockery of our plans, our achievements and even our virtues and good deeds. They will not survive.

But, in Christ, we will. St Paul tells us that 'if for this life only we have hoped in Christ, we are of all people most to be pitied.' We are dust, but remember, though dust is our end, it is also the material of life-giving creation.

In John's Gospel, the raising of Lazarus is the seventh of the 'signs,' starting with the wedding feast at Cana, that Jesus gives to show who he is. Seven is a biblical number for wholeness, since God's creation of the world reached its fulfilment on the seventh day. The fulfilment of Jesus' mission is found in the raising of the dead. That is really what the Lord is all about.

'I am the resurrection and the life,' says Jesus to Martha and to us. 'Those who believe in me, even though they die, will live, and everyone who lives and believes in me will never die. Do you believe this?' When we make or renew our baptismal commitment, we are asked the same question: 'Do you believe in . . . the resurrection of the body and life everlasting?'

What is my answer? I say, 'I do,' but is that merely a gesture on my part? Do I really live as if I were convinced that nothing, not even death, need terrify me with the threat of abandonment by God? Am I convinced that death, fearsome though it be, is a 'sleep' for one who has been baptized into the life of the risen Lord?

We will soon celebrate the resurrection of Christ. That is our joy and our hope. Today, before we are overwhelmed with that celebration, we recall that his resurrection involves us as well. Just as Lazarus was called from the tomb, we know that in some way or other we, too, will be called by the Lord to new life.

All we know about Lazarus is that his sisters loved him and that he had friends. One of those friends was Jesus. In our Baptism, I accept the Lord's offer to be that kind of loving friend to me. He will do for me what he did for Lazarus. I will return to dust, but I believe that one day I will be called: 'Come to me!'

Palm Sunday (A)

The night I saw the film *Schindler's List* about a man who schemed to save Jews from the Nazis, I did not sleep well. I kept wondering what I would have done if I had been there. Would I have done evil? Would I have cooperated with it? Would I have tried to not be involved? Would I have resisted quietly with low-grade subversion or at least disloyal, though unspoken, thoughts? Would I have opposed it, even if it meant death?

Today we involve ourselves in the events of the week in which Jesus was executed. In the Palm Sunday liturgy, we identify with various ways of responding to Jesus on his journey to the Cross.

We begin the liturgy as supporters, bearing palm branches and singing hymns. Within 15 minutes or so, we cry, 'Crucify him!'

Perhaps some of the people who demanded Jesus' death at the end of the week had begun the week singing hosannas. Who knows how or why they changed? Perhaps their 'Hosanna' was not sincere. Perhaps their 'Crucify him!' was not sincere. Perhaps both were sincere.

What would I have done? Would I have gone along with the crowd? Would I have stayed a silent spectator to 'Jesus' Joyride' as well his Way of the Cross? Would I have opposed either the praise or the punishment? Like my dilemma over the Nazis, I don't know or fear to know the answer.

It is fairly easy for most of us to say we are Christians, especially if we do so in moderation. Sunday Mass? Generally okay. Renouncing a promising career because of what it does to the world or to my spirit? Crazy, but somehow admirable. Denouncing the values of my family or society because they have become life-destroying idols? 'Crucify him!'

Today, I am forced to take both sides, to 'try them on for size.' I cannot avoid a decision, saying it only applied to people in Jerusalem long ago. I wave the palms and cry out for the death here and now.

Of course, in the liturgy, we are only play-acting. Or, are we? The choice to be an open follower of Christ or a Sunday-morning Christian or a betrayer is before me all the time.

Most of the choices I make are not life and death issues. They are compromises and corner-cutting that getting through life entails, like crying 'Hosanna' or 'Crucify' because everyone else is doing it or the script calls for it. No major decision, no major commitment.

That's frightening. Could it be that the 'little' betrayals that define my life are, when combined with the 'little' betrayals of others enough to send Jesus to the Cross? One small voice saying 'Crucify' would not have done much. A crowd of small voices brought Jesus to Golgotha.

When we meditate upon the Cross, we must look upon our sinfulness without providing excuses for ourselves. I am a sinner who needs redemption. I may not think of myself as a great sinner, but even my 'little' sins, my *ad hoc* refusals to live as a child of God, my momentary inattentiveness to the consequences of my actions or inactions toward God and my neighbor are sin.

In Holy Week we recall that God's love does not merely redeem the world from its sin, but even redeems me from my own 'Crucify him!'

Easter Sunday

Japanese Christians have a wonderful greeting for this day. They say *gofukkatsu omedetou gozaimasu*. The phrase means 'Resurrection, congratulations!'

When do we congratulate others? Obviously, when something wonderful has happened in their lives.

By saying 'congratulations,' I say I share the other's joy. It's an unselfish greeting. 'Congratulations' refers to the other person and the event's meaning for him or her, not so much to the event itself.

What is it for which Japanese Christians congratulate one another? 'Resurrection.' But, why should we congratulate each other for what happened to Jesus? Isn't it he who deserves the congratulations? He is the one whose rising we celebrate. What have you or I to do with that?

A lot, as it turns out. On Easter we do not celebrate the Resurrection of Christ as a once-upon-a-time event. It is our feast as well as Christ's. You should be congratulated on Easter and should congratulate your fellow Christians as well because in Christ's Resurrection, we, too, are raised to new life.

That is the reason that during the Easter Mass we renew our Baptismal commitment. As St Paul reminds us, in Baptism we enter the grave with Jesus in order to be raised with him to new life. So, on the day we celebrate Jesus' rising to new life, we reconfirm our union with him.

This day new life began for all of us when Jesus rose from the dead. Easter is our birthday in eternal life.

When does eternal life begin? When we die? Yes, but not at the death we usually think of, our physical death. Eternal life began for us when we died with Christ in Baptism and entered into union with the risen Lord. So, the day we renew our Baptismal promises is in a real sense a celebration of our birthday. Resurrection, congratulations!

Christ is risen, and we are risen through him, with him and in him. So what? Is my life really all that different from that of others because I'm baptized? Am I more moral than others? Nicer than others? Better than others? Not particularly.

So, what's the point?

My biological life does not, for the most part, depend upon my conscious choices. I do not control the way my organs work. My life in Christ, however, requires some response on my part.

On Easter, we recommit ourselves to that response. We renounce a life apart from God and declare our desire to live as sons and daughters of God. We make a choice to live eternal life here and now. That, too is cause for rejoicing. Resurrection, congratulations!

What will this commitment mean to me and the world? It should mean freedom from the fear that prevents my accepting and sharing the love of God. If I am already living eternal life, why fear anything that can happen to me in this world?

I am united with the risen Lord. So, I can be a servant to God and my neighbor. I can be the sign of the new creation begun in the Resurrection of Jesus. Resurrection, congratulations!

Easter is the anniversary celebration of your new birth in Christ through Baptism. It is the day on which eternal life became available to you through his Resurrection. It is the day you renew your commitment to living that new life for God and the world.

Resurrection, congratulations!

Second Sunday of Easter (A)

Years of living on the streets of Tokyo had taken their toll and the man needed hospital care. The doctor at the voluntary clinic asked me to accompany the patient to the welfare center to ensure that they would arrange hospitalization for him. It was only a few blocks away, and he could walk that far.

As we took a shortcut through an alley, the man suddenly started frantically brushing his body with his hands and screaming, 'BUTTERFLIES!' He was hallucinating, and saw and felt that his whole body was covered with butterflies.

'There are no butterflies here,' I said.

'Can't you see them? They're even all over you!' he said.

'No, there are no butterflies on either of us.'

'Are you sure?'

'Yes.'

Then, that man paid me possibly the greatest compliment I have ever received. He believed me. He still saw butterflies, he still felt butterflies. But, in spite of all the evidence, he decided to trust me when I said there were no butterflies.

Some fools like Thomas in the Gospel say that seeing is believing. 'Unless I see . . . I will not believe.'

There is a bit of Thomas in all of us, but I think that man in Tokyo is a better example of what we are like. To believe in Christ is to trust in spite of a lot of what we see and feel.

This is Easter time. We proclaim that Christ is risen. We say that God's love has overcome the power of sin and death. We say that the power of evil is broken.

Yet, when we check the news we see that evil seems to have survived the breaking of its power. Whenever I look into my own heart, I see very clearly that sin remains alive and well there. Injustice continues, and suffering is universal. Disease, disaster and death destroy without regard for the innocent or sinner, the believer or nonbeliever. The same liturgical books that contain the prayers of Easter contain funeral Masses as well. No sane person I know has met Jesus walking down the street.

There can be no doubt about it. The evidence that Jesus was God, killed yet now alive, is hard to find. Rather, the evidence makes a good case that either there is no God, or if there be one, God does not or cannot care for us.

And yet, we Christians keep singing alleluia. Are we crazy?

That is possible, and an honest Christian should from time to time face the question of our sanity. Facing it will help us to have a faith that can live in the real world, rather than in some realm of self-created make-believe.

In addition, since our vocation is to proclaim Christ as the answer to the world's doubts, fears and woes, we had better be ready to honestly face those doubts, fears and woes ourselves. If we don't, our proclamation will be unbelievable to those who live with the bad, rather than the Good News.

But, let us assume for the moment that we are not crazy. Let us assume that we are like that man in Tokyo, turning from craziness to reality in spite of what we see and feel.

He believed my vision of reality because he was willing to trust someone of a different nation and race. He made a decision about me and about how he would understand reality.

Is that similar to my faith in Christ? What I know of him has been told me by a community of his disciples called Church. And, I choose to trust that community and the One of whom it speaks. I choose to accept their vision of reality in spite of all the evidence that says that we are alone in this world without any loving God caring for us.

Thomas did not trust that community. Not believing the Church, he could not see reality.

In the final analysis, it becomes a matter of choice. I can choose to trust the Church and Him of whom it speaks. That choice, like that of the man in Tokyo, will be based upon an inkling that this community is interested in my good and will accompany me on my journey, risking the fact that it may, in fact, be mistaken and covered in butterflies itself.

Third Sunday of Easter (A)

The Gospel only names one disciple on the road to Emmaus, Cleopas. There is no reason, then, to assume, as artists and others invariably do, that the second disciple was another man. Perhaps the disciple was a woman—Cleopas's wife, for example.

It would be suitable for the second disciple to be a woman, because theirs is not a 'once-upon-a-time-in-a-land-far-away' tale. It is about us, men and women who struggle to understand and believe in Christ.

The first notable thing about the disciples is that they are not paralyzed by the frustration of their hopes about Jesus. It is the third day since those events, but already they are on the road, getting on with their lives. That does not mean that they have forgotten Jesus, or that they ignore reports that he has risen. As they walk along, they keep him in mind and in their talk.

We, too, carry on our day-to-day lives. Sometimes we feel disappointed in our hopes. Sometimes we wonder about the value of our commitment to Christ. But, we still get up in the morning and go through our day. We must, because just as the disciples met Jesus on the road, we, too, will meet him on the road. Our daily lives are the place where faith is explored, questioned and ultimately confirmed.

The disciples talk with each other about Jesus. When the stranger joined them, they continued to talk about him. They talked about Scripture. They talked about what Jesus had said and done. That was not enough.

Some Christians think it is sufficient to hand Bibles to people. The experience of the two disciples should be a caution for such believers. Information about Jesus, conversation about Jesus, theological statements about Jesus, or even the best explanations of Scripture will not bring people to faith. Something more is needed.

So, the disciples continue on the road to Emmaus, still talking about Jesus and through his explanation coming to a deeper understanding of Scripture. But, they still do not, cannot, really believe. Faith does not depend upon information.

The basis of faith is an encounter with Jesus Christ. Understanding the Scriptures and the teachings of the Church can and should help us toward that encounter, and we should continually grow in our understanding of them, but they cannot replace the encounter.

Where does the encounter take place? Here we come to the core of Luke's message today, in what the two disciples say about their experience. 'They told about how he had been made known to them in the breaking of the bread.'

They had walked with him, but could not believe. They had talked with him, but could not believe. They had listened to him, but could not believe. But, 'when he was at the table with them, he took bread, blessed and broke it, and gave it to them. Then their eyes were opened, and they recognized him.'

From that Sunday to this, we followers of Jesus break bread and in that action know that the Lord is risen and is with us. The Eucharist proclaims the Resurrection.

When the disciples recognize the Lord and realize that the rumors of a 'vision of angels who said that he was alive' are true, 'He vanished from their sight.' Once they realized that the Lord had been with them all along, they no longer needed to see him with eyes of flesh; the eyes of faith see better.

'That same hour they got up and returned to Jerusalem' where they told the others of their encounter. They became missioners, proclaiming the Resurrection of the Lord. That is the only appropriate response to their encounter with Jesus.

That, too, is our story. We share the Eucharist, and in that sacrament we know that the Lord is with us on all our roads, at all our tables. Then, we go to share that Good News with all. A Christian's encounter with Jesus is always meant for the sake of others.

The way we share that Good News is the same way that Jesus shared it with those disciples. Just as he walked with them in their sorrow and confusion, we walk with our brothers and sisters in their sorrow and confusion. Just as he joined them in their meal, we join others in their everyday lives. Just as he shared with them the Word of God and the Bread of Life, we offer them not only the fruits of our encounters with Jesus, but the opportunity to experience that encounter themselves.

Fourth Sunday of Easter (A)

In ancient Palestine, shepherds frequently kept the village sheep penned together at night. That way, the shepherds could take turns on guard and all could get some rest. In the morning, each shepherd would call his own sheep, and they would come to him, following him to the pastures.

There is a special relationship between a sheep and its shepherd. The sheep knows the shepherd. On his part, the shepherd knows the sheep, even recognizing them as individuals to whom he gives names.

Our relationship with Christ is similar. He knows each of us as individuals, not merely as part of a flock. He addresses us each by name. He knows me because he loves me. Because of that love, he watches me because, like a shepherd, he wants to protect me and lead me to good pastures.

There is one true shepherd, Jesus, and many false ones. In John's Gospel, this section is presented as an attack upon Jewish leaders of his day. If that were all it were, it would have little meaning for us today.

However, it is likely that the evangelist included this passage in his Gospel because the Christian community for which he wrote was experiencing problems with false shepherds, those who would lead the community astray. That problem is not limited to the Christians of long ago.

We use the word 'shepherd' in the Church quite often. However, since we use it in a Latin form, we might not recall that we are speaking of a shepherd when we say 'pastor.' Those who care for the Church and have responsibility for leading it exercise a 'pastoral' ministry. They are shepherds, responsible for protecting and leading the community.

In the fullest sense, pastors are not solely bishops and the priests who are appointed by them. All who lead, heal and nurture the faith of a Christian community exercise, in various ways, a pastoral role.

Theirs is a heavy responsibility, since they must imitate the Good Shepherd who knows his sheep and loves them. It is a responsibility with great temptations to exercise power rather than service, to receive special treatment rather than to give without seeking return and to seek fulfillment of one's own physical, psychological or spiritual needs at the expense of others.

We probably all know men and women who have turned away from the flock of Christ because of the actions or inactions of some 'shepherd.' Sometimes, these men and women merely use a shepherd as an excuse. But, sometimes, they really have been driven off by someone who acts more like a wolf than a shepherd. Others do not leave the flock, but carry wounds inflicted by bad shepherds, wounds which they may have forgiven, but which leave scars anyway.

We must pray for those bad shepherds. We must pray for those who have been hurt or driven off by them. And, in our prayer, we must be willing to be used by God to be the instrument of healing for shepherds and sheep alike.

We must also encourage and thank good shepherds with our words, prayers and actions, and be examples of willing cooperation with them for the sake of the entire flock.

Often, however, we sheep are to blame for being led astray by bad shepherds. The sheep of whom Jesus speaks in the Gospel can tell the difference between their own good shepherd and a bad one. We are not always so discerning.

We follow shepherds merely because they hold some title. We follow shepherds who tell us what we want to hear. We follow shepherds who make us feel good. We follow shepherds who will relieve us of the responsibility to make choices for ourselves. Sometimes we even choose men or women as our shepherds who do not want to be so in the first place.

The solution to both problems—unworthy shepherds and willingly misguided sheep—is to know the true shepherd, to 'know his voice.' If we know the Lord, we will recognize false shepherds and will also know when we are searching for false shepherds.

And how will we learn to recognize his voice?—by knowing Scripture, by deepening our understanding of his Church, by prayer, by gathering in his name, by sharing the Eucharist and by imitating him in his love of God and people. If we do that, we will recognize his voice and follow when he speaks through real shepherds.

Fifth Sunday of Easter (A)

My sympathies are with Philip: 'Lord, show us the Father; stop the fine words and give us something we can understand. Make it easy for us to believe and we will believe.'

The disciples two thousand years ago had trouble understanding. We disciples today still have that problem.

Actually, as is so often the case, the evidence we seek is under our noses. In fact, the evidence follows our noses wherever they go. We are the evidence that there is reason for faithful confidence in Christ.

Obviously, the basic place where I dwell is myself. It is also the place where Christ dwells, because in Baptism I have become one with him. Jesus has gone to the Cross and returned to us, as he promised. In the Father's house called the People of God, there are many dwelling places. Since the Father and Jesus are one, wherever he is, there is heaven.

However, looking at the world, at the Church or at myself, can I actually say, 'Here is heaven'?

Yes, I think I can. The words of Jesus that we hear today are from his discourse at the Last Supper. So, as Jesus headed to torture and death, he spoke of being 'the way, the truth and the life.' Apparently, the presence of heaven on earth does not preclude the possibility of evil, of suffering or of death.

To understand this, it is necessary to understand something about the theology of the evangelist we call John. Something that takes place for Luke in the Ascension happens on Calvary for John. For him, the Cross is Christ's glorification. So, in preparation for his Passion, Jesus says, 'The hour has come for the Son of Man to be glorified.'

It is impossible for me to understand how God allows suffering in the world. I can admit that generally my 'suffering' is rather less than terrible when compared to that of others. But, no one's suffering is insignificant to that person.

Much of what I undergo in life is, in fact, my own fault. If that were the only sort of suffering, I could see some sense in it, a sort of therapy for my weakness and sin. However, there is much undeserved suffering in the world.

In fact, suffering seems to be one of the basic realities of life where so much of life depends upon the ingestion of other creatures. We kill and eat to live.

So, suffering in its many forms is the story of the world. (Not the whole story, of course—there are also love, friendship, good humor and other graces.) Perhaps what Jesus tells us today is that in the midst of this story, God is with us, sharing divine power with us that helps us not only endure but also to turn our disaster into triumph. 'I tell you, the one who believes in me will also do the works that I do and, in fact, will do greater works than these.'

We do this through the Spirit, the Spirit that is present with us no matter where we may be, no matter who we may be and no matter how many of us there may be. Jesus was limited in his ability to be with his disciples. Only a small number could see him at any time because he could only be with a small number at any time. The limitations of time and place that hem us in hemmed him in as well. But, his going to the Father means that the Spirit of God is among us. Wherever we go, whatever we endure, God's Spirit is with us. Heaven is with us.

That should be enough, but there is more. Jesus was the presence of the Kingdom in the world, and the Holy Spirit is the continuation of that presence among us. But, our story here has an ending. We all die. The world itself will die.

Saint Paul reminds us that 'If for this life only we have hoped in Christ, we are of all people most to be pitied.' We are citizens of the Kingdom of God, united with Christ in Baptism. But, we also pray for the coming of that Kingdom, for its fullness. The Kingdom is something in store for the world, but also something in store for you and me.

Jesus tells us today that the place where we live with God is not only this world we live in now. He has prepared another place for us, one with 'many dwelling places,' enough dwelling places for each of us to live with him in his Father's house.

Sixth Sunday of Easter (A)

The Greek word 'paraklētos' that we translate 'Advocate' was a legal term meaning 'one called to stand beside.' The function of such a person was to support someone standing before a court—in other words, an attorney.

Why would Jesus speak of sending an attorney? Is following Jesus illegal, that we need fear being hauled into court? Well, that has happened, and for many Christians the thought of having the Spirit of God as an attorney beside them has been a source of courage and hope in the face of persecution.

But what of most of us Christians? Are we likely to stand before judges to defend our faith?

As a matter of fact, yes, even though the judges do not sit in a courtroom.

Peter's letter tells us, 'Always be ready to make your defense to anyone who demands from you an accounting for the hope that is in you.'

Why would anyone demand an accounting for my hope? Obviously, the reason would be that they had seen hope in me.

What does hope look like? How would someone recognize it, and how would it be enough of a characteristic of a Christian that others would want to ask about it?

The place to look is hopelessness. Hope in the midst of hopelessness raises eyebrows, questions, doubts and sometimes even ire.

In the Easter season we rejoice that the most hopeless situation, the death of God, is the way to eternal life. This hope in hopelessness is the reason the Cross is the symbol of our faith.

It is not hard to find hopelessness today. There are wars and violence. There is poverty, injustice and disease. Our environment is being altered in ways that may cause irreversible damage to the planet and life on it, including ours.

More real to me is hopelessness in my own life and the lives of those around me. Friendships fail. Dreams decay. Love is lost. Death awaits us all. Even my good desires and hopes are dashed 'for I do not do the good I want, but the evil I do not want.'

In the midst of all this, to talk and act as if there were reason to hope does raise questions, sometimes even in myself. I must stand before accusers who say, 'Get real; you are a deluded fool who refuses to live in the real world.'

What, exactly, is our hope? It is not that our little dreams will be fulfilled. Nor does it mean that our most desperate prayers will be answered as we wish. Christians' prayers at the bedside of a dying loved one do not seem to have a greater 'effectiveness' than prayers of those who are not disciples of Jesus.

Our hope is based upon the very same Spirit that Jesus promises to send to us. The Advocate who will give us the means of answering for our hope is itself our hope. 'You know him, because he abides in you, and he will be in you.'

Because the Spirit of the Risen Christ is in us we can face our own crosses with confidence that God is still at work, that God's will is done even when it is thwarted, as it so often is.

Since we have that hope, we can love the 'unlovable', forgive the 'unforgivable' and do without the 'essential.' That provokes interrogation by the world: 'Why do you have such hope in you?'

The answer is that Christ the Lord is risen and with us so intimately as to be in us. 'On that day you will know that I am in my Father, and you in me, and I in you.'

The Lord is with me, so there is no reason to despair, to not hope. My own hopes and dreams may collapse around me, but compared to the fulfillment of the hopes and dreams of God, that collapse is a minor affair. Disappointing, but not crippling.

Hope does not mean that we assume in the face of the facts that all will be well with the world. It does mean having confidence that even when all is not well, we are not abandoned by God.

It also means committing ourselves to living as if we believe it, so that others may ask us to give a reason for the hope that is in us and thus give us an opportunity to proclaim the presence of God the Holy Spirit with us.

Ascension (A)

People are fascinated by last words. There are even books that collect them. Among my personal favorite parting words are those spoken by a general during the American Civil War to soldiers who were taking cover from enemy snipers: 'They couldn't hit an elephant at this distance.' Perhaps not, but in the absence of elephants, they could hit a major general.

One reason for our fascination with parting words is that they sometimes summarize the life of the speaker, whether that speaker is dying or simply leaving for someplace new. That is especially true when the speaker has had time to think out the words ahead of time.

Sometimes, the words that are passed on are not actually those of the person to whom they are attributed. Others invent words after the fact to provide inspiration, entertainment or a fitting tribute to one who is gone. Such are the last words attributed to Mother Teresa, 'Jesus I love you. Jesus I love you,' and some variants on that. According to an eyewitness, her actual last words were, 'I can't breathe.'

To conclude his Gospel Matthew gives us a version of the parting words of Jesus. Like parting words that summarize the speaker's life and work, Matthew has thought them out and intends them to summarize his Gospel.

He begins by having Jesus declare his credentials, reminding us that it is important to pay attention to what the Lord has to say. He says that all authority in heaven and on earth have been given to him. In other words, what he commands is not only trustworthy, it is to be obeyed.

And then, he gets to the important part of the message. 'Go, therefore, and make disciples of all nations.' The Lord does not command reflection, prayer or worship. He commands action. His disciples are to get moving. All else is secondary to that and is meant to aid that. Reflection, prayer and worship should help us better go to the nations.

In Scripture, 'the nations' are not countries like those whose flags are lined up in front of the United Nations headquarters in New York. The nations are Scripture's way of speaking of those who do not believe, those who are not yet part of the People of God. Jesus tells his followers to go to them, to make those people the focus of the Church's activity.

In fact, they are the reason the Church exists. Just as the Son was sent into the world by the Father, the Church is sent into the world. The reason we exist as Church is for the sake of those who do not know Christ, and to the extent that we focus our attention, service and concern toward ourselves, we are not really being Church.

Too many people do not know of the love of God. Most of them believe in some god or religion or other. Some even claim to be Christians. But, their understanding of God is not based upon a conviction that God is love, and therefore they still need to hear the Good News from true disciples. Others are doubtful about who God is. Yet others deny that there could be any God at all.

There is only one way that they are going to learn the truth about God who is a loving relationship among Father, Son and Holy Spirit that overflows as love for us. That way is for disciples of Christ to teach them what Christ has taught us, that God so loved the world as to send the Son to be our savior.

We are to do that in such a way that attracts followers just as Jesus did in his ministry. Our service to God and our sisters and brothers should be such as to draw others to join us through baptism into the death and resurrection of Christ. Then, they, too can proclaim the Gospel to all nations.

There are many obstacles to our doing that. The world often seems uninterested in hearing the Good News. Sometimes, like the disciples who were with Jesus on the mountain, we ourselves doubt. At other times, our sin and weakness interfere and make our proclamation seem more like bad news or empty words.

However, we must not give up hope nor must we give up the proclamation. The Lord assures us that in his glory he is no longer limited by time and place and is with us today and always. That assurance gives us the confidence we need to obey his great command.

Seventh Sunday of Easter (A)

There are many ways to keep the word of God. One is to get a Bible. We might even go so far as to read it.

The Church keeps the word by making Scripture a part of our worship. The Church also passes the Scriptures on from age to age. We study them, reflect upon them and quote them. We use them to guide our lives. Sadly, we sometimes abuse them to find individual texts that 'justify' what we, rather than God, might want.

All that is probably the most basic, and in many ways, the least demanding way to keep the Word of God. It is focused on the word of God as we find it in Scripture.

But, when Jesus spoke, there was no such thing as the New Testament. Even what we now call the Old Testament was still not formally organized as it is today.

So, when Jesus prayed, 'they have kept your word,' he was not referring to texts. He was speaking of the word as the will of God, a will that we learn in the pages of Scripture, but not solely there.

Scripture and the guidance of the Church can give us informed hearts in order that we might perceive the will of God as it is found in the two most important places. The first is, of course, in the teachings, actions and attitudes of the Word made flesh, Jesus Christ.

It is not enough to know *about* Jesus. In Scripture, prayer and reflection, we must come to know him as our teacher, our model, our companion and our savior. We must develop a sense of how he would live and act today in our circumstances.

The second important place to learn what it means to keep the word of God is our own experience. The Spirit of God is at work in the world, and we must do as Jesus did, using our faith, hope and love to discern the will of God.

We are in the world as the presence of Christ for today. 'I am in the world no more, but these are in the world as I come to you.' Since Jesus lived in a different age, we cannot expect that imitation of his acts alone will be appropriate to our age. We trust in the Spirit that he has sent us for guidance and insight.

Saint Pope John XXIII misused a phrase from Scripture but gave us keen advice when he told us that we must 'read the signs of the times' to see what God calls us to today.

What are those signs of the times? Some are positive. Many aspects of human life have improved greatly. The growing concern for human rights is a positive sign for those who believe that God's word calls for a communion of brothers and sisters, children of one God.

However, some signs of the times are not so positive. Yet, they give us an indication of the will of God. The history of the past century has been marked by unprecedented violence that has forced us to recognize the power of sin in our lives. We have been horrified into reflecting upon the kind of world God intends.

The world as it is has not yet become the world as God intends it to be. We are sent to show what it should be by being keepers of God's word.

In today's second reading, Christianity is contrasted with behaviors that we can assume in any age and any place do not keep the Father's word. Three—murder, theft and evildoing—are fairly straightforward.

The fourth is hard to translate, and the wide range of translations gives us a broad idea of the behavior that Christians and their societies should avoid: 'concealer of stolen goods,' 'spy,' 'informer,' 'mischief maker,' 'intriguer,' 'busybody' and the one that may sum up all the others, 'destroyer of another's rights.'

However we translate, it is obvious that Christian behavior is contrasted not with sins 'against God,' but sins against our neighbor. In the Incarnation of Christ, the place to obey the Word of God is, above all, in daily life.

So, we should examine our lives and commit ourselves to living as those who keep God's Word. That will often mean going against the ways of the world, including when those ways have found a home in our own hearts or in our own Church.

Pentecost (A)

What does it mean to say someone is 'at home'? If we are talking about sitting within reach of their doorbell, we mean the person has not gone away. To be at home in this sense also means a readiness to welcome visitors.

It is possible to be 'at home' without being home. I can be at home at the address of a friend. I feel comfortable, welcomed and loved. My host is glad of my presence, but without fuss. The refrigerator door is mine to open.

If someone invites me to be at home, it is not the sort of 'at home' I enjoy or endure at my own place. I have moved, have gone away from my own home to enter another's. To be at home in this case means abandoning my own 'at home.' In other words, when someone makes me feel at home, I am not at home.

The two kinds of 'at home' are mutually exclusive. Either I am home at home, or at home away. I cannot be welcomed to my own house, nor can I be at home at another's without moving.

Pentecost is an 'at home' day, reminding us that God is at home with us and we with God.

In what sense of 'at home' is this true? Is God 'at home' at some divine residence, awaiting our visit, or has God entered our home? Are we 'at home' in our world, or are we welcomed in God's home? Who is the welcomer? Who is the welcomed?

God is separate from creation. In other words, God is not at home as a native of the universe. Yet, we celebrate the fact that God has 'moved in.' The Holy Spirit has taken up residence in our world. It is God's home.

So, we are invited to be at home in God's own home—not just a heaven beyond place and time, but in this world. We live in the house of God, God's welcome guests.

But, it is our home, too, and we can invite God to be at home. How? Well, what makes good hospitality? First, the welcome itself. We should be aware of God's coming to us and rejoice in it. Beyond that, like good hosts, we should do whatever it takes to make our guest comfortable. When that guest is God, hosting means not preparing favorite foods, but doing what Christ has told us is pleasing to God. That is, loving our Guest and all in the house—every child of God.

So, God hosts us and we host God. What about the guesting? When God joins us as guest, what happens? When guests come, they often bring a gift. In the Pentecost Gospel, Jesus presents a gift, the power to forgive sins. When God gives a gift, it is not like some of the gifts that guests bring, good only to be hidden away somewhere. God's gifts are meant to be used. We must be forgivers.

And what of ourselves as guests? What does it mean to be told by God to make ourselves at home? Feeling at home in the world is difficult. Very often, it seems like an unwelcoming place. It can be cold and threatening. Many men and women are fearful of the world. They feel unwelcome in it.

That is why this feast of the Holy Spirit's coming is so important. Since God is at home in our world, welcoming us as guests, we can live without undue anxiety. We have been invited to make ourselves comfortable here.

What does it mean to be comfortable in God's world? What are the spiritual equivalents of refrigerator privileges? One is the right and ability to pray. We can turn to our host and ask for what we need.

Even more basic is the right to feel at ease. When we make ourselves at home in another's house, we may hear all sorts of unfamiliar noises at night. But, knowing our host, we are confident and comfortable. In this house of God we call our world, there are many things that can disturb us, but we continue to live with confidence in our host.

Pentecost reminds us that God is at home in our world as our guest. It also reminds us that we can be at home in the world as God's guests.

Trinity Sunday (A)

There is no way human minds can enclose the One who created them. Even so, it is good for us to reflect upon the mystery of the Trinity from time to time so that we can grow in knowledge and love of the One who loves us more than anyone else.

One meditation upon the mystery of the Trinity focuses upon that love. St John tells us God is love. In the Creation of the world and of each of us, in the Incarnation of Jesus, in the Cross and Resurrection of Christ, we see that confirmed. God is love without limit, love without prejudice, love without thought of return.

Love is something that gives of itself. A man's and a woman's love for one another is a nurturing, life-sharing gift. As fellow human beings, each is able to receive the fullness of the other's love and return it. The nature of love is mutual sharing.

Now, if God is love, where is that mutual sharing? The love God has for me and the rest of creation is so great that it gives us life, even eternal life. Yet, it is not mutual because there is no way I can love God as God loves me. If God is love, there must be something about God's self that makes the fullness of love, mutuality, really present. Otherwise, something is missing, inadequate, in the love of God. That mutuality is the relationship in the One God between the Father and the Son.

However, there is more to love than mutuality. There is creativity. When a man and a woman love one another, one expression of that love is in the creation of new life. Through the mystery of sex, two people bring a third into being. Mutual love finds its fulfillment when the lovers turn toward a third and share the mystery of their love for one another. This is a hint of the mystery of the Spirit, the third Person of the one God. The love of the Father and Son finds its completion in their sharing it with another who loves them in return, the Spirit.

The love of each Person in the Trinity is infinite, unstinting and absolute. It is infinitely equal in each, and therefore infinitely equal in all. So, the three are one.

These reflections may illuminate the mystery of the Trinity, and may even be an aid to prayer and faith. If they are not, forget them. The Trinity is true; the explanations are shadows of shadows of the truth.

But, if we grant that this meditation on the Trinity has some validity, we should look at it to see what implications it might have for our own lives. After all, if we are created in the image of God, then there must be something about us that at least parallels the mystery of the Trinity. A deeper appreciation of that mystery should teach us about what it means to be a human being.

So, where do I find the mystery of the Trinity in my life as a child of God?

Though my father was dead at the time, we celebrated my parents' 50th wedding anniversary because it was not only the anniversary of two people's marriage, but was the anniversary of the birth of a family. That man and woman eventually shared their love with children, making the one family a unity of several persons. One reason marriage is a sacrament is that it is in some ways an image of the life of God, the Three-in-One.

So, besides being a feast on which we reflect upon the mystery of God's love, perhaps this a day for all of us, especially those of us who are married, to reflect upon how our love for one another should be unselfish, unstinting and, within the limits imposed by our weakness and sin, unbounded.

Do I really share love with others, as the Father shares love with the Son? Is our mutual love a source of grace, life and love for others? Am I, are we, concerned for the well-being of all God's creatures? In other words, do I imitate the Trinity in my living and loving?

We are created in the image of God who is love. That love finds expression in a threeness in oneness in which the mystery of love overflows beyond the limitations imposed by mathematics and human understanding. So, Christians called to show God's love to the world should show a love that is so full as to overflow us, bringing unity to a world of many persons.

The Body and Blood of Christ (A)

Our Eucharistic celebration preserves actions that once served practical purposes. During the Middle Ages, some of them were misinterpreted as allegories. So, the priest's washing of his hands after the gifts were brought to the altar was seen as a re-enactment of Pilate's washing his hands of responsibility for the crucifixion of Jesus. In fact, the origins of the hand washing are more prosaic. In the ancient liturgy, the priest washed his hands because they were dirty.

If his hands were dirty, why didn't he wash them before the liturgy? The problem was that they were dirtied during the liturgy, during the presentation of gifts.

I once celebrated a Mass in Nigeria where the gifts went far beyond the—to me—usual bits of bread and wine and possibly the money collection. This offering included a goat that looked and acted willing to charge me. Folks more used than I to dealing with goats held it back while with a city boy's nervous scrutiny of its horns and teeth I laid a hand on its head as I had been told to do. I also accepted dirt-covered yams and other vegetables and fruits as well as a few chickens. The hand-washing afterwards was more than a symbolic gesture.

Offerings in the ancient Church were more like that one in Nigeria than many of us are used to. The members of the community offered bread, wine and other foods and gifts. The bishop or priest would accept all of this, and then take only a bit of the bread and wine, barely enough for everyone present, and put the rest aside for distribution later to the poor. Then, he would wash his hands.

So, the bread and wine that became the Body and Blood of Christ was part of the service of the Church to the poor. The Eucharist is a communion with Christ first of all, but, in Christ, also a communion with the community of believers and with those whom the community serves.

St Paul reminds us, 'Because there is one loaf, we who are many are one body, for we all partake of the one bread.' (This was much easier to comprehend in the pre-host days when, in fact, one or more loaves were broken and shared as the Eucharist.)

Each celebration of the Eucharist is a declaration to the world that the People of God are united in Christ. How often do I recall this fact when I am celebrating the liturgy? Desultory singing, half-hearted responses, daydreams, judgements on fellow worshipers, rehashing of old arguments and theological or catechetical mind games—all sorts of things go through my lips, mind and heart during worship. Most of them detract from, rather than building up the Body of Christ we call Church.

I am willing to admit that the Mass is a proclamation of unity among those sharing the action, a sign of union with the whole Church and a re-commitment to serve the world. The problem is that when I look around me at the real men and women who are supposed to be one, I often allow myself to be separate from them. I would rather pick and choose those with whom I am 'loaved.'

Fortunately, Christ is not so choosy. He is willing to be present in the bread and wine that his people share. He is willing to be present in that people and in what they do as individuals and a community to show the love of God to the world. It is his real presence in the sacrament that makes us really a community and really able to serve.

That union with one another in Christ for the service of the world is our foretaste of the eternal life to which we are invited. 'The one who eats this bread will live forever,' says the Lord. By being 'loaved' with one another in Christ, we become heaven on earth.

This is the link between our celebration of the Eucharist and our mission to evangelize the world. Our liturgy is a sign that Christ calls us all to unity. It is an experience of that unity. It is a unity that is meant to be carried beyond the walls of the church to the whole world, since the whole world is the source of the fruits of the earth and the work of human hands from which we make our offering.

CPSIA information can be obtained
at www.ICGtesting.com
Printed in the USA
BVHW072037301219
568186BV00001B/45/P